"Luci Shaw has spent a writing lifetime finding thumbprints in every square inch of creation and then pressing down more than a few for us to discover on our own. The glory of the prints she explores in this new collection of essays and occasional poems is attributable to the hand of the Creator. But what Luci does in *Thumbprint in the Clay* is what she always has done for the rest of us: she teaches us to see."
James Calvin Schaap, author of *Reading Mother Teresa*, *Up the Hill*, *Romey's Place* and *Touches the Sky*

"What a delight when someone has something really good to say, and then says it with such style and grace. Such is Luci Shaw! She sees and describes the divine thumbprints well."
Richard Rohr, OFM, Center for Action and Contemplation

"Luci Shaw is a friend, seasoned soul and wise 'lady of letters' who writes 'from the edge of the known world.' Her inspired, enlightened, well-crafted essays guide us toward recognizing the marks of the maker in everyday life as she illustrates on each page how to take 'a long, loving look at the real' and find God there."
Dick Staub, author, broadcaster and founder of The Kindlings

"Luci has thrown clay upon a wheel yet once more and fashioned it into a delightful vessel filled with my favorite drink: the ambrosia of art, faith and creativity. Yes, I am besotted, but who can turn away from the poetry of a life lived so beautifully in service to God?"
Leslie Leyland Fields, author of *Surviving the Island of Grace*

"Luci Shaw is a treasure, and *Thumbprint in the Clay* shows us yet again precisely why: this book is wise beyond measure, the writing beautiful beyond compare, and its heart a reflection of the one true God. We see the evidence of Christ everywhere around us, and yet we seem determined at times to overlook his proof. This meditation allows us to pause, ponder and bring close to our hearts the fact of God's design, his love and his purpose for our own lives. This is a beautiful, ruminative and necessary book."

Bret Lott, director, MFA in writing, The College of Charleston, author of *Letters and Life*

"What a joy it is to see life again through Luci Shaw's artistic vision. *Thumbprint in the Clay* is marked by the particular beauty of her ingenuity—wisdom kilned into her through years of fully engaged living, poetry that flows forth from her creative magnanimity, and her attuned, sensuous awareness of hints of the Creator's presence in every nook, niche, name and soul that kneels before the Holy. Shaw invites us into the God-imprinted adventure of incarnate life, not a 'narrow destination.' Illuminated by this book, we see that the imprinted life is an experience of penetrating mystery and indelible grace."

Susan S. Phillips, New College Berkeley, author of *Candlelight* and *The Cultivated Life*

Thumbprint in the Clay

DIVINE MARKS OF BEAUTY, ORDER AND GRACE

LUCI SHAW

IVP Books

An imprint of InterVarsity Press
Downers Grove, Illinois

Also by Luci Shaw

Poetry

Listen to the Green
The Secret Trees
Postcard from the Shore
Polishing the Petoskey Stone
Writing the River
The Angles of Light
The Green Earth
Waterlines
What the Light Was Like
Harvesting Fog
Scape
New and Selected Poems (forthcoming)

For Children

The Genesis of It All

With Madeleine L'Engle

Wintersong
A Prayerbook for Spiritual Friends
Friends for the Journey

Nonfiction Prose

God in the Dark
Water My Soul
The Crime of Living Cautiously
Adventure of Ascent

InterVarsity Press
P.O. Box 1400, Downers Grove, IL 60515-1426
ivpress.com
email@ivpress.com

InterVarsity Press® is the book-publishing division of InterVarsity Christian Fellowship/USA®, a movement of students and faculty active on campus at hundreds of universities, colleges and schools of nursing in the United States of America, and a member movement of the International Fellowship of Evangelical Students. For information about local and regional activities, visit intervarsity.org.

Scripture quotations, unless otherwise noted, are from the New Revised Standard Version of the Bible, copyright 1989 by the Division of Christian Education of the National Council of the Churches of Christ in the USA. Used by permission. All rights reserved.

While any stories in this book are true, some names and identifying information may have been changed to protect the privacy of individuals.

Portions of this book were previously published in Luci Shaw, "Imprint: Thumbprint on the Clay," CIVA (blog), December 17, 2010. Used by permission.

The poem on p. 51 is "The Blue Eyeball" by Luci Shaw. Copyright © 2006 by Luci Shaw. Published in What the Light Was Like *(WordFarm, 2006). Used by permission from WordFarm.*

The poem on p. 65 is "Tenting, Burr Trail, Long Canyon, Escalante" by Luci Shaw. Copyright © 2006 by Luci Shaw. Published in What the Light Was Like *(WordFarm, 2006). Used by permission from WordFarm.*

The poem on pp. 194-195 is "Potter God" by Randy White. Published in Poetic Intercessions: Artful Prayers for a Friend *(Harmon Press, 2010). Used by permission.*

Cover design: Cindy Kiple
Interior design: Beth McGill
Images: andipantz/iStockphoto

ISBN 978-0-8308-4457-9 (print)
ISBN 978-0-8308-9390-4 (digital)

Printed in the United States of America ∞

Library of Congress Cataloging-in-Publication Data

Names: Shaw, Luci, author.
Title: Thumbprint in the clay : divine marks of beauty, order, and grace /
  Luci Shaw.
Description: Downers Grove : InterVarsity Press, 2016. | Includes
  bibliographical references.
Identifiers: LCCN 2015050898 (print) | LCCN 2016001645 (ebook) | ISBN
  9780830844579 (pbk. : alk. paper) | ISBN 9780830893904 (eBook)
Subjects: LCSH: God (Christianity)--Omniscience--Meditations.
Classification: LCC BT131 .S53 2016 (print) | LCC BT131 (ebook) | DDC
  242--dc23
LC record available at http://lccn.loc.gov/2015050898

P	17	16	15	14	13	12	11	10	9	8	7	6	5	4	3	2	1
Y	30	29	28	27	26	25	24	23	22	21	20	19	18	17	16		

To Tim, Karen, Mike and Ron,

fellow scribes who have imprinted me

for good and God

Contents

The word that came to Jeremiah from the LORD:

"Come, go down to the potter's house, and there I will let you hear my words." So I went down to the potter's house, and there he was working at his wheel.

JEREMIAH 18:1-3

Preface

*E*vidence is everywhere. Hints. Clues. And our calling is to be detectives. To notice. To respond.

Paleontologists uncover fossils and learn about ancient forms of life. Archaeologists dig to uncover remnants of civilizations that have been layered over in succeeding centuries. We learn a great deal about an ancient people from their pottery, their tools, their metal work, the shards of their lives, the ways they decorate their bodies and their belongings. It is all evidence that needs decoding.

Perhaps you've been reading about the destruction of ancient archaeological sites, demolished because they are considered idolatrous by an invading army. Though these physical evidences—temples, statues, mosaics—of human belief and worship are glorious and valuable, marks of creativity and culture, they are considered by some worthy only of destruction. Communities of witness record their beliefs, hoping they will survive. The Chinese terracotta soldiers. The Mayan temples buried in the Central American forests. The pyramids and their hidden tombs for pharaohs. Stonehenge. The testament of history is not easily obliterated or ignored.

Say we notice a series of large paw prints in the snow crust along the highway up to Mt. Baker in the state of Washington. We pay attention, reminded that this is mountain lion territory. Or the wound of scraped-off bark left on a tree near our wilderness tent reminds us that we live in proximity to other created beings. Some large creature has left its mark—evidence that we share space with other members of God's creation. We become aware of our surroundings by attentiveness, relieved that black bears and human beings prefer to keep their distance and need to respect each other's boundaries.

Wherever there is life it leaves evidence like the paw prints of the cougar, the rough scrape from a bear paw on bark, the writings and artifacts of human history.

There is also a spiritual dimension, an unseen but very authentic reality that will alert us to evidence beyond our senses. We call it transcendence, or the supernatural. God's Spirit is powerful enough to change the way we see the world and respond to it.

We may find ourselves in an ancient church or cathedral, and as our attention is drawn to the Gothic arches, the buttresses, the altar, the font, the nave shaped like a boat and its pews (that remind us of our rowing toward God), the stories illumined in the brilliant stained glass windows, we begin to realize that every detail is significant, planned and placed to remind us worshipers of unseen realities. And holy space is made more holy by our sacramental worship, our partaking of wafer and wine. Our passing of peace within this community of grace.

None of our doings and beings are meaningless. And because we human beings have eyes and ears and perceptive minds, we draw conclusions about the evidence we see, whatever information we can deduce. Our senses allow us to observe and consider and sort and differentiate, picking up significant clues, leading us to certain conclusions. And our art or poetry brings them into cleaner focus.

In this book I've made serious attempts at decoding some evidences for purpose and design and beauty in our created universe. This is our planet and here we are, integral parts of a system rich with evidence. These clues lead me to believe in a Creator who leaves his prints on our environment, our history and our personal lives. Our challenge is to be aware and invite God to speak to us through the fabric of what is made, what has happened, inviting our enthusiastic response, our co-creating with our Maker.

one

Coffee Mugs

*I*t is a Northwest morning, early.

As yet the sun is below the horizon, but pale, lemon-colored light is filling the sky like a bowl. I glimpse it through our bedroom's skylight. I stir under the sheets and wonder about getting up. At length, a finger of low winter sun stirs me into wakefulness, and an almost instant response rises to my mind. In my gown and slippers I go downstairs. It is the air, ambient with the smell of coffee brewing, that has invited me into this day.

From our kitchen window I have a view of Bellingham Bay, its water gleaming up at us from below our hill. It seems to be viewing me just as I am seeing it, a sort of mutual inspection. Watching that glancing light on the water speaks to me of how reciprocal perception enriches life. But within the house other intrigues call me strongly.

It's not just the coffee, already brewed by my ever-earlier-rising husband. Nearer at hand, on the wall opposite the window, is a double row of wooden pegs, twenty in all, each holding a mug as if grabbing a friend by the elbow and saying, firmly, *Hang on tight, this is where you belong.*

The mugs don't match; they are not meant to match. Their diversity is part of their aesthetic appeal. There are sixteen of them, each so individually itself and yet finding its perfect resting place in the company of others. A little community of blues and greens and aquamarines and a touch of earth brown in one, not only useful but beautiful to me; they enhance the color schemes throughout our living space. I grab one, cross the kitchen to the coffeepot and pour, adding half-and-half and sweetener to my taste.

Aah, the perfect start to any day. The possibilities are endless. I have a new poem going, a dentist appointment, a gift to buy for a friend's wedding. Church choir practice in the evening. But it's my morning cup that gets me in gear.

Somehow, the satisfaction of really good coffee is enhanced by the beauty of the coffee mug. And all around my house, on shelves and windowsills and pegs, I have what I regard as a fabulous collection of hand-thrown pottery—mugs but also fruit bowls, salad bowls and jugs, a small curved tray, a planter with its flowering occupant, each formed with its own subtle earth tint or glazed jewel tone. Each makes its use appealing, whether for serving, storing, holding, pouring. Or just looking at with enjoyment. These days when guests arrive, I invite them to choose from the rack a mug for coffee or tea, and their choice tells me something about them and their preferences. The tea bags themselves—English breakfast, Earl Grey, peppermint, chamomile, chai, ginger—wait on the counter in a sage-green pottery casserole dish with a cover that I bought at a flea market years ago.

Each of these pieces of kilned earth has a history. Back in the sixties in Illinois we had a family friend who was a skilled potter. Richey made for us a hundred mugs with the name SHAW in raised letters on the side, each to be given to any bookseller who placed a significant order. (This was while we had our own independent publishing company and went to the annual trade show to publicize our authors and sell our books.) The mugs, with different colored glazes, were popular bonuses, and we had some brisk sales as a result. I still have a couple of those mugs, one brown, one deep blue. My children each have their own—reminders of when the family would drive to Denver or Texas or Chicago for the booksellers' conventions.

I love every member of this earthen family, the look of them, as well as the feel of the shape and texture as I hold each in my hands. Their familiarity is part of their charm. This morning I am comforted and motivated for the day's work as I breathe in the caffeinated aroma rising in the morning from a favorite mug (though it's hard to pick one; they're all my favorites!).

Each piece, whether it's a mug, a mixing bowl, a milk pitcher, a vase, a turkey platter, a serving dish, is the result of combining earth and human eye and muscle with individual design, skill and intense heat. Some of these treasures are hand built, some shaped on the potter's wheel, many bearing the thumbprint signatures of the potters themselves or their names or logos scrawled on the mug handle or the bowl base. Having that personal identifying mark makes a piece of pottery memorable to me. It's as if the maker is proclaiming his unique identity, saying, "Don't forget! I impressed this mark in the clay before firing to let you know it is authentically my artifact, and it will always be personal, from me to you."

In the 1950s, in an effort to relieve the academic pressures of college term papers, I enrolled in a ceramics class. I produced some primitive bowls and vases on the wheel, and that introductory process triggered my fascination with the art. I remember the cool, damp, firm slabs of clay we were given and the wonderful messiness that went into the process of building a pot. I can still almost feel the water-moistened clay and slip on my fingers as the wheel revolved. Manipulating clay on the wheel is absorbing and sensuously fascinating. Its immediacy and fluidity satisfied the craftsperson in me; under the hand and fingers, and with sustained pressure as the potter's wheel turned, something shapeless and almost embryonic rose into a recognizable shape.

As the object takes form, with glazes and decorative incisions, and is finally placed in the kiln for firing, the excitement grows. Will the completed piece fulfill my expectations? Or will it crack when I remove it from the heat of the kiln and allow it to cool?

Perhaps God, the original artist of the universe, looks at each of us, his human creations, the work of his loving artist hands and heart, with the same intense anticipation. We are living proof of the Creator's skill, and we hope we bring him not only usefulness but gratification!

As I've traveled, I've collected decorative pieces with the distinctive mark of their maker on the bottom or the name of the town from which they have arrived. These identifying marks can be seen only when the piece is lifted and inspected. There's the large blue, black and white platter from Iznik (Nicaea), in Turkey, with an intricate geometrical pattern all done (almost miraculously) by hand. And pottery pieces, their traditional patterns cunningly and artfully inscribed in black on white or ocher clay, from a visit to the Acoma pueblo in New Mexico. Also from the Southwest, I've purchased, at considerable cost, several subtly shiny pots in the tradition of the great Mata Ortiz, baked underground in dung to turn them black and then traced with smoky black emblems that reflect the Native American cultures. I have terra cotta from Mexico, stoneware from Portugal, porcelain objets d'art from Ontario, the Netherlands, Tennessee, Romania.

A saucer with "Tonala" in blue script on its base came from the Mexican hamlet we were driving through when our car was badly damaged from being run off the highway by a truck. We were stuck there for days while our vehicle was being repaired. I broke a rib in that encounter, but I love the miniature bowl I bargained for at a roadside stall and use it still for guacamole!

I own a few "rejects," some pieces with a slightly flawed shape or a crack from firing, creations that didn't meet the high standards of the artisans, who sold them to me at a discount. But they are still useful and valuable to me, reminding me of the continued value of imperfect, somewhat damaged goods. Like many human beings. Like me.

I can visualize the setting in which I found each unique piece. I remember which artisan I purchased it from and when—that Galiano Island potter in his workshop in the backwoods whom I discovered twelve years ago, the friend who died suddenly last year just after he'd removed his fired pieces from the kiln, the thank-you gift of two earth-brown mugs from a friend in Scotland, my brother-in-law's raku pots fresh from his kiln on Bainbridge Island, the salad bowl from Old Jerusalem ("Lady, you my first customer today. I give you special price!"). Each of these treasures brings to mind the setting of its origin—a boutique in a small Ontario town inhabited by artists or an art museum or a resale shop.

I have a vegetable dish that broke when I dropped it; I glued it back together with Elmer's, loath to relinquish it to the trashcan. Somehow it has since resisted twenty-five years of dish washings and still offers its charming, ancient self to hold fruit on my kitchen counter.

The why of my choices is nearly always implicit in the piece itself, the aesthetic appeal or shape or function that corresponds to my need, my impulse, my desire. I don't go for pretty or highly decorated or delicate. No flowers, please. No happy faces or cheerful phrases or jokes designed to put me in a jolly mood. I'm particular, persnickety. I know just what I want, and I go for it.

Once I received a gift mug from the organizers of an arts conference at which I'd spoken and given a reading. The gift card read, "To the lady of letters," and the handcrafted mug was engraved with the letters of the alphabet around its blue-glazed belly. Though I didn't choose it myself, its message is so apt, and it always reminds me of the high-octane weekend with a community of like-minded writers and readers who'd marked my presence with them in a distinctive way and somehow understood my taste in pottery, which meant that maybe they understood *me*! It's still a loving reminder that takes me back to them.

Each of these pieces of shaped and decorated clay is an example of a kind of incarnation—a unique physical expression of the human potter's skill and artistry. As with any art form, a reflection of the artist's soul is embodied in that individual's creation. It reminds me of God's own identity as a potter that is marked in Scripture in four separate passages. This is the God who injects in us his own magnificent creativity and appreciation of the beautiful. When we cultivate this aptitude for making something beautiful, we are adding our own prints on that which our Creator has freshly printed in us.

I sometimes ask myself about beauty, arriving as it does in such variety, taking so many diverse forms. Why is it that everywhere on our planet we not only create useful things, but we decorate them and shape them according to our culture or our individual taste? Practicality is not our only value. Its design enhances any object's worth. Perhaps it's because a perception of beauty, and a deep longing for it, is part of our human essence, enfleshed in each of us by a Creator for whom beauty is an act of grace?

Conclusion? Beauty is Love taking form in human lives and the works of their hands.

two

The Faces of the Earth

*T*he thumbprint on the curve of a mug handle is for me a singular clue to human identity. Testing this manually I think I've figured out why: a thumbprint leaves a more powerful impression than a fingerprint because there is a greater weight of hand and wrist, bone and tendon behind it. My opposable thumb is especially useful because it also allows me to grasp an object (a railing, a coffee mug, a steering wheel) in a way that would be difficult, if not impossible, for my four fingers alone.

And those are only two of the reasons this image of a thumbprint carries such energy for me. At work on my computer keyboard, it's my right thumb that thumps the space bar, moving the words and ideas along the line of type. Texting a message to a friend on a smart phone is tough for me; my fingers have grown too knobby and bent from arthritis. But for most of the population I'm sure that thumbs are intimately involved as words are transmitted by means of the tiny keyboard of some electronic device.

Just as each human thumbprint is unique, its pattern inscribed on the work of our hands and minds, the Creator's is even more so—the original thumbprint on the universe. It can be seen in the whorls of suns and planets in space, in the nebulae, and closer to home in the fractal patterns of tree branches and roots, in the formation of crystals in geodes and diamonds, frost and coal. Just yesterday, after an icy winter night, I recognized divine design in the intricate, unrepeatable arrangement of frost crystals, tiny sparkles, precise sunbursts and starlets and coronas with the sun shining through them, decorating the glass panels along our deck. I photographed the frost before it melted and transferred the exquisite image to my computer's screen saver. I love these visual reminders of what I have seen and found entrancing. And I love how I can save them in living color and beauty, thanks to technology.

On one of the daily Internet postings by Fr. Richard Rohr (I find in them nourishing food for daily meditation and divine guidance), the headline read, "Bearing the Divine Fingerprint," followed by a quotation from Job: "Everything bears the divine fingerprint, footprint, or similitude." The man Job, caught between the demands of Satan and the will of God, in his response to Zophar's taunting, struggled with life's meanings, his own life's meaning, and responded: "Ask the animals, and they will teach you, or the birds in the sky, and they will tell you; or speak to the earth, and it will teach you, or let the fish in the sea inform you. Which of these does not know that the hand of the LORD has done this? In his hand is the life of every creature and the breath of all" (Job 12:7–10 NIV).

The view from a plane at 36,000 feet, through air unobstructed by clouds or haze, gives us a newer, wider grasp of earth patterns, with their meandering crest lines, their lakes and branching waterways. And even as I fly home from a distant speaking engagement and the plane begins its descent, the contours of Washington State's Cascade Mountains and its complex coastline grow clearer; its islands and inlets, spits and beaches coincide with my internal map of home. And then, below us, Bellingham's streets glimmering in the streetlights come into view and let me know how close I am to landing. I have been imprinted with their familiarity.

The patterns repeat: the Frio River in the Texas hill country near San Antonio has deposited lime along the riverbed in odd and wonderful configurations carved by water over the years. It is possible to drive along the shallow lengths of the river as on a paved highway. I get a shiver of excitement as my car proceeds along this watery way. On Facebook my photographer friend Bob Denst posted an image of a trickle of water winding its way down a beach, carving its own miniature, meandering channels in the sand as it drains down into the ocean. The braided rivers of New Zealand's South Island, their currents twisting their way around pebbled islands of bushes and mosses, remind me of the way wisteria vines twine around and grow into each other, and that in turn brings spirals to mind. A convolvulus vine "revolves" as it climbs a trellis. A snail shell unfolds in a precise mathematical sequence (known as the Fibonacci sequence). As does a nautilus shell. The water scrolling clockwise down the bathtub drain. The upwinding of the human life, and the outgoing, ongoing expansion of the universe.

It seems evident to me that some superhuman hand once set in motion geological movements that formed the crests and fissures of mountains and valleys. And deserts, with blazing circles of green that show human activity in irrigating dry wastelands, turning them into fruitful fields, moisture enabling the latent nutrients in the soil to stimulate verdant growth. Water and weather may be artistic tools or destructive forces. In either case, powerful agencies for change.

As is common for many artists, Georgia O'Keeffe relished earth patterns—the contours and colors—dramatically translating them into her paintings. I've been overwhelmed as I've viewed her versions of the New Mexico landscape in all its variations. When I visited the museum in Santa Fe that celebrates her life of art, I learned that in a flight around the world in the forties O'Keeffe made pencil and charcoal sketches of what she saw from a plane window over the vast stretches of Asia. She was intrigued by the way rivers were sculpting the landscape far below. The fractal patterns caused by the erosion of the rocks and mesas—the mountains and valleys and deserts with their purple and sage shadings—profoundly influenced her painted landscapes. Her dramatically large canvases of colored flowers and animal skulls have a sensual quality typical of her work. She invited the land to speak its beauty to her eye and hand.

At home I have a favorite tangle of dried kelp, not formed by human hands. I found it stranded high on one of our Bellingham pebble beaches, shaped by wave action, propelled by a high tide and dried by summer sun. It looks intricate, two cunningly intertwined lengths of brownish seaweed fiber with their seed pods still attached. I picked the thing up and carried it home, and here it hangs, suspended from a nail on my office wall, artful in its naivety. Friends look at it and wonder. I tell them I liken it to my gastric and reproductive systems (including my ovaries).

For many artists, and even for an amateur photographer like me, such geological or botanical formations are almost irresistible! They are like God's graphics. The rimed bubbles of air trapped under the clear window of ice over a mud puddle in an Illinois winter have made me pull to the side of the road and stop my car, crunching through vestiges of snow to capture them in the lens. I've photographed the tracings of veins in a leaf backlit by sunlight. And the way the colored leaves pattern themselves on the ground as they fall in fall. The ghostly, unrepeatable swirls of smoke rising from a snuffed candle, obedient to the invisible drafts of air. The whole earth is imprinted with patterned intricacy. I see the fingerprints of the Creator with eyes that have been formed by that Creator with the ability to recognize meaning in beauty, to notice and be informed and enlivened.

In New Mexico and Arizona, previous civilizations have left their unique marks on rocks and cliffs, bearing witness to past events by means of symbols. Driving with my friends Karen and Nicola across the high desert, we come upon the sudden fissures, profound cracks in the flattened plain, of Arizona's Canyon del Muerto and the Canyon de Chelly. (Willa Cather described them as "cracks in the floor of the world."[1]) These declivities fork off into separate branches carved over eons by rivers flooding into gulleys hundreds of feet deep. They snake through the red rock wilderness, aptly known as the "Painted Desert" for its rich and varied earth tones—intense copper, cinnamon, madder, carnelian, turmeric, ocher, warm pinks and grays and browns. Rust and ivory. Bone and blood. Ridged and stippled and layered sandstone in astonishing formations, all irresistibly intriguing. The chasms' sheer cliffs are stained with vertical ribbons of the bloodlike minerals leached from the earth above and painted there by rain. They remind me of enormous wall-hanging tapestries.

Water winks from the streambeds that weave along the canyon floor, edged with piñons, junipers, cottonwoods, sagebrush. It runs alternately as a trickle or a flood, depending on local cloudbursts or droughts.

It is an early summer morning. Yesterday we'd driven from Albuquerque, New Mexico, east into Arizona, where the highway forks northwest into the Navajo reservation. With the sun just beginning to send its arms of light down into the valley, we begin an excursion into the shallow end of the spectacular Canyon de Chelly. At first it is just an arroyo, a minor dip in the surrounding wasteland. In the height of this summer we give thanks that it is still cool, with a light breeze. We are seated in an open-bed truck driven by a Navajo guide (this is Navajo country and we are here having paid a fee and been given a permit to enter their protected domain). He has made sure that we are equipped with water bottles and broad hats for shade.

On the plastics seats, once cushioned, now worn flat, we bump along. After a mile or two, the cliffs begin to rise higher on each side and the canyon deepens. The sun follows us all morning, gaining strength as it arcs in the indigo sky, pouring its blaze into the valley. There is no breeze. We begin to sweat, fanning ourselves with our hats and tippling our water bottles.

Here and there, where the canyon widens along the pebbly river's edge, bordered with juniper and water willow, the local Navajo women, who have climbed down the cliffs from their reservation on the flatlands above, have set up display tables for their wares. We inhale the incense of cedar wood burning in a primitive oven and realize we are already hungry. They sell us fry bread and Pepsi to wash it down. They invite us to examine their handcrafted jewelry, turquoise, coral, bone and silver, and a table of hand-thrown pottery laid out in a splendid array. We stop to look, feel, lift, choose. Each piece is charming, beautifully made, unique.

After Karen buys a string of pale turquoise beads, I cannot help myself. At one of the tables managed by a woman with a smiling, bronzed, creased face, I bargain (but not too severely; this is how this woman makes a living) for earrings, a necklace. I have a connection with her. The pieces of jewelry and the way they have been designed speak so fervently about our common human capacity to create beauty, adornments, from whatever raw materials are available—rock and metal and horn and shell, turquoise and coral. For me it is most often word pictures, scraps of verbal art. We are both printed with the desire to make beauty out of whatever is at hand, physical, spiritual or emotional, that arrives in gleams from beyond us.

Back in the truck, in the scorching heat, we keep driving for hours. Occasionally we stop for a breather in the shade, inhaling the moist odors of weeping rock under an overhanging cliff, until we reach the gorge's end, covering over forty miles, stopping often to take note of where the Anasazi, "the ancient ones" of previous civilizations, have left traces of their activities. Stretching sharply up, piercing the blazing blue sky, are the rocky monoliths that were long-ago refuges against assault, scaled by women under attack, with their infants on their backs. We see the faint notches in the perpendicular walls where they would clamber up to safety when attacked by warriors from another tribe or rapacious Spanish invaders.

All this is heaven for a photographer! We employ our cameras madly as the truck lurches along over sandbars or through running water left from a downpour the night before. We note the shimmer of sunlight on ribbed wet sand, bordered by green cottonwoods, or the shape of a single white cloud in the blaze of blue sky, an image worthy of Galen Rowell. Every angle is a kind of icon that burns its likeness into our minds; as the light shifts, what seemed unremarkable a minute ago reveals itself as striking, magical, unique.

Perspiring, panting with heat and almost exhausted with admiration, we come to a stop at the far end of one canyon for lunch and step down from the truck onto the red soil, patched here and there with tough, low-growing thorny chaparral. It has been a jolting ride on hard seats. We stretch. We thirstily gulp water from a cooler and rest under the shade of an enormous cottonwood, like a grandfather tree, whose exposed roots spread out wide around it, creating their own knotty and intriguing patterns as they grip the ground and suck up the sparse moisture. My eye is alert for such configurations. I find them wherever I look. I take series of photos to memorialize this ubiquitous phenomenon of aesthetic need and supply.

There, at the canyon's end, we have reached a vantage point where we can look up and marvel at the pale, clay-colored cave dwellings built high above the valley floor under the shadowy overhang of the tawny cliffs. These enclaves are protected, fenced off along the base of the cliffs. We're not allowed to approach too closely; these are remnants of civilizations that must be protected and preserved. No modern graffiti, no intrusive explanatory signs, but our guide is a fount of information as we pepper him with questions, explaining, pointing out different features of this people's ancient history, culture and way of subsistence. We maintain our distance, using our zoom lenses to bring us closer, trying to imagine how native families would live, high above the valley floor, with such limited access to crops and water. These cave dwellers' lives were carved by primitive need and supply, by vulnerability and security, and by their desire to print their lives on their environment.

Their pictographs and petroglyphs are visible, scrawled high on the cliff walls and sandstone surfaces. We are only able to examine them through our binoculars. Our guide explains that they often represent feudal clashes with other ancient peoples. Though we might call the stick figures primitive, the drawings are also recognizable as hunting or agricultural scenes. Depictions of cattle and deer. Human figures on horses. Corn stalks. Spears and what look like shields. But among them, scratched onto the stone and still distinct, some symbols for peace and prosperity show up clearly. The flourishing (or poverty) of these people's lives was printed on the rocks for us to see and wonder about in our own time and culture.

A Teton Sioux proverb goes like this: "A people without a history is like the wind on the buffalo grass." Such efforts to record something of human lives that will not be obliterated are to be found throughout succeeding civilizations on our planet. Like nearly all human beings, these ancestors of today's pueblo peoples didn't want their lives to be forgotten or erased. And they are not. Through the clues they left in the form of dwellings and drawings, archaeologists and anthropologists have learned an astounding amount of detail about how the early inhabitants met their challenges to survival.

It's the day after our truck trip along the canyon and back. We drive up out of this massive split in the landscape and motor along the winding canyon rim, hundreds of feet above the dusty trail and the shining filament of water winding in and out of shadow along the valley floor below. We stop at several pullouts labeled by the Arizona Highway Authority as "Viewpoints." Seeing the same valley from the height allows a new and different perspective, a stereoscopic understanding of both geology and anthropology, in much the same way that two angles of sight combine to become three-dimensional. We see the patches of cultivation—a couple of clay and wattle hogans and scattered patches of corn, as well as the neon green cottonwoods and tamaracks that lined the serpentine reaches of the river. We needed the ground level to notice details up close, but the sweeping contours of the valley can be observed clearly only from the heights. Eagles can see it all. We wish for eagle eyes for ourselves, and sometimes a cliff edge or a plane window will do.

And then I remember an all-seeing Eye looks down on us as well—us and our world—and notices the marks we leave in our living, sometimes overriding them. But sometimes refining and affirming them.

three

Beauty

Its Shapes and Signs

Where I live, very happily, in the Pacific Northwest with its moderate climate and good people, we are close to Puget Sound and Bellingham Bay, our intricate inlet from the sea. Beyond it, beyond the complex jigsaw puzzles of the islands, lies the vast ocean. Our shores are bordered by tall evergreens and smooth-pebbled beaches and above them the lovely surprise of uprising sandstone rocks. (For Annie Dillard these shores represented "the edge of the known world" as she saw it, peering out over the Pacific Ocean, and preparing to write the history of this sweeping land and seascape in her book *The Living.*[1])

I sit on a sun-warmed sandstone shelf in Whatcom County's Larrabee State Park, overlooking the Sound. The ripples on the water catch the sun and send their tiny light flashes, like signals. I can feel the grit of the friable sandstone under my hand. The rocks arch over me like breaking waves, carved into intriguing crannies and hollows, and pitted with a kind of stone lace where wind and water have whirled tiny fragments of sand within multiple concavities until the rock face becomes an example of pure, abstract art. At water's edge, a different art shows up where the tides lift and withdraw; a cluster of white barnacles has found purchase at tide line. I take photo upon photo, angling each shot differently. It is impossible to find an ugly viewpoint. This is where air, land and water meet and mingle. The waves send a glancing radiance onto the rocks and barnacles, and clear tide pools make watery art with the sea stars and rounded pebbles of sea glass (that are sometimes called "mermaid's tears").

After a while I've exhausted the camera's battery, but it's okay. I've caught and breathed in enough of the glory of the ancient and the present to fill me. It is enough for now. For me, these shorelines bear divine thumbprints, like the multitudes I can see almost anywhere, if I pay attention. It all speaks to me with palpable reminders of ongoing creation, and formation. We have a God who creates and re-creates as if our world is a park, a divine playground in which we are invited to join the games.

Soft Rock

You need only to live near mountains
to feel the age in your bones. Take
the sandstone cliffs along our Northwest shore:
looking across pebbled beaches glinting

with sea glass, their faces staring down the ocean,
never as pacific as it sounds. These bluffs
have offered themselves without rest to
the winds, the waters — rising, falling fifteen feet —
the extraordinary tides, rips that tear
water from water, that scour the shores.

On this windless day, I feel joined to
the low shelf on which I sit. Warm
from noon sun, it's pitted into stone lace
by particles whirled by wind for a million years
in the rocks' shallow wounds. Any small grit
will do it, grinding at the stone face, digging deeper,
carving empty eye sockets.

Lines of barnacles like white dried flowers
grow at the waterline, footnotes
to weather's virtuosity.

No one is watching.
Surreptitiously I lean left, touch,
test with my tongue the etched boulder
by my elbow, and taste the sharp salt of storms.

In that brief kiss I think I even sample
the ochre-gray tint of sands that once
laid down their duned lives
to become these rocks of ages.

Rocks speak their own silent but eloquent language. And along the shore the multiple pebbles in a range of colors and textures, still damp from a high tide, each tells its own story of being chiseled and shaped by seawater and movement and continued rough contact with each other.

But how infinitely more complex are our human means of interaction! Our complementary human genders, our succeeding generations and cultural contexts—each has a distinct and distinctive history, a narrative, an identity, a character, a personality, a way of seeing the world and a way of expressing what we have seen and heard. We communicate, share, give out and take back, making war to protect our assets or assert our power, but also making art and making love. We are as varied and intricate and striking as stars or snowflakes. As internally rich and complex as geodes. Or seeds that hold compacted within themselves all the components of growth that burst into new leaves and flowers. Carl Linnaeus was able to sort these colors and shapes and growth patterns taxonomically and name them—a boon for the botanists that follow him and rely on his classifications. And we human beings? We're as different as Eve was from Adam, and as they both were from antelopes or elephants or eels.

What a gift is particularity. And peculiarity! The uncommon, the distinctive, the unusual. I love the King James language in which Peter tells us that we are chosen by God to be "a peculiar people" with a special role in God's economy. And I have come to believe, through observation and reflection, that when all the particulars are found on one planet, creating diversity, every instance of beauty and variation that results is God's way of injecting grace into creation. I believe, with Richard Rohr, that every creature is a word of God, a way of expressing the value of that individual, that God loves diversity and makes of his entire creation a letter that he signs with his own fingerprints.

I've also concluded that beauty doesn't reside simply in *what* we observe, or *the fact* that we can see and take note, but in *how* we perceive and distinguish, with all our senses.

I'm convinced that it is in juxtaposition, in relationship, in design, in contrast and comparison and pattern that we discover beauty and meaning, building on *what is there, available*, as we move forward into originating new beauties and meanings. Further, that we, as responders, are called on to create in the image of our Creator.

Have you found, as I have, that *beauty* is a word that seems to escape precise definition? It's tough to try and define beauty without getting all squishy and sentimental. It's never mere prettiness or comeliness or attractiveness. It often involves bold light slashed across with dark shadow, as in Renaissance chiaroscuro. Commonly held understandings of true art vary with the culture of multiple historical periods or movements or schools. You may prefer Botticelli to Kahlo, or Vermeer to Modigliani, or Gauguin to Warhol. All I can say is, "To each his own"—there's so much generosity in it; the possibilities are infinite! Each style or technique brings a dollop of divine generosity into view through the lens of an artist's eye and imaginative interpretation. From there it achieves focus, turns more and more real on canvas or film or wood or stone. Often ambiguity ("What does it mean?") is part of its appeal, challenging us to live with it for a while and investigate it further.

And always there's a quality about visual or verbal art that elevates it out of the ordinary. When I use the term *beauty*, I'm not referring simply to harmonious melodies or a young girl's fresh prettiness, or to the kind of pro forma sentimentality found in a greeting card or a popular romantic song, or the physicality to be seen in a Miss Universe contest.

Here's my own take, my personal attempt to define my perception of the beautiful: it's an echo of the true, the angle of light on an object that reveals it for what it *is*, intrinsically, in a kind of naked integrity. It's a perception that involves both seer and the seen. It takes us as partners in revelation to bring beauty into view. It may shock us out of our conventional concept of aesthetics by revealing an original aspect of reality. Gerard Manley Hopkins came at the diversity of beauty through his poet eye:

All things counter, original, spare, strange,
Whatever is fickle, freckled, who knows how?
with swift, slow, sweet, sour, adazzle, dim,
He fathers-forth whose beauty is past change. Praise him.[2]

Clearly Hopkins, a Catholic priest and visionary, viewed creation as God's artwork.

I'm convinced that in the Genesis 1 narrative, as God is surveying what he has created, calling it "good" and "very good," he was saying with enthusiasm, "Just *look* at all this! Isn't it *beautiful*?"

In a sense, beauty—any category of virtue or verity—may be redemptive. It can enliven our spirits, inspiring us (and the word *inspired* really means inspirited—breathed into by the Spirit of God).

I watch for beauty in the experience of what we might aptly call *glory*—the appearance of something of such supreme worth that it begins to make sense of all the breakage, the heartache and distress of our world.

I find it intriguing that the Hebrew word for glory embraces the idea of weight, heaviness, volume, worth. It's not the kind of flashy performance or quality that may excite us in the moment (though we'd guess it is too trivial to remain with us). Glory, holiness, has an unearthly substance. Though

it may be momentary—it's often a glimpse of something won-
drous, capable of evoking our wonder—it changes and chal-
lenges something deep within us. I love what John Calvin said
in his commentary on Psalm 19: "The glory of God is not
written in small obscure letters but richly engraven in large
and bright characters, which all . . . may read, and read with
the greatest ease."[3]

One year I spent some days on silent retreat at a monastery
on the coast of California. It was spring, and the whole world
glistened with freshness. I'd driven down from Washington,
from my home north of Seattle, tent-camping in heavy fog
on the northern California coast along the way and then, as
the fog lifted, following the Redwood Highway south through
San Francisco and Monterey to the spectacular Big Sur. It's a
coastline that outlines the Pacific coast with a series of steep
cliffs that thrust up like eyebrows over the ocean.

The monastery is seated high on one of these cliffs over-
looking the Pacific. Driving up from the highway below, I
followed the dirt road's loops and turns up and back and forth
across the cliff face, the ascent almost a pilgrimage in itself.

My time alone, booked with the Hermitage months before,
was to be spent in one of the tiny, rustic trailer guest cabins
nestled into the greenery just down the steep decline of the
precipice, below its brow. Above me, outlined against the
bluest of skies, stood the Hermitage Chapel with its bell and
cross. No fog. Nothing to obscure the astonishing clarity.

Beyond the chapel, among pepper berry trees, were the cells where the monks lived and studied and prayed, following the rule of St. Romuald, an eleventh-century Benedictine saint and founder of the Camaldolese order of monks. This is one of his directives: "Sit in your cell as in paradise. Put the whole world behind you and forget it. Watch your thoughts as a fisherman watches for fish. . . . Realize that above all you are in God's presence, and stand there as if you stand before the king. Empty yourself completely and sit waiting, content with the grace of God."[4]

For months I had been leading a very active, productive life following my calling as a writer. I've come to believe what poet Paul Mariani was driving at when he said that "your craft is your spiritual discipline."[5] In other words, if God has blessed you with a gift, exercising your gift as a trust given you by God is the way to please him. I'd been writing assiduously out of this sense of responsibility, all the while feeling spiritually dry and apathetic, unsatisfied because though much of what I was doing was supposed to be God work and was in service to God's people, I'd felt a disconnect, a lack of *feeling* that I was in touch with God himself. I longed intensely for something beyond my limited self to be drawn toward, to cling to, to be touched by love.

Distraction and the disruption of overactivity are the enemies of creative work and spiritual vitality. In such times I know I need an uninterrupted time devoted to silence and solitude so that I can settle down, begin again to focus, listen for a Voice, adopt an internal posture of waiting, and hope to become more aware of the Presence that is so deeply missed and longed for.

Seeking without finding lasting certainty had been a constant in my spiritual life, and in times of discouragement it has seemed an evidence for me of lack of faith, producing an ensuing guilt and sense of failure. The only solution for me, too often delayed by my responsibilities, busyness, is to get away from the urgencies of ordinary life and spend time in solitude or silence. That may take the form of either driving across the country on my own (I've done that a couple of times in the Southwest, allowing the open reaches of landscape and skyscape to calm or lift me) or sitting in my wilderness tent with Bible and journal, surrounded by forest and stream. Or, in what I want to tell you about, at a place designed for retreat such as the Hermitage north of Santa Barbara, with food and shelter provided so that I don't have to worry about the exigencies of living.

A place where God can get at me, fix his gaze on me, and I cannot turn away.

The destination itself involves a kind of pilgrimage. I'd driven down, more than a thousand miles, south along the West Coast through Washington, Oregon and Northern California, largely along the glorious Redwood Highway and the Big Sur with its magnificent cliffs that mark the western edge of the continent.

This monastery and its refuge offered such an opportunity for connection or, rather, reconnection. Following Eucharist the day I arrived at the retreat center, I'd spent time in silent meditation in the chapel. A white-robed monk was the only other person, seated across the sanctuary from me, silent, head bowed. In that sacred interior space, where so much praise and worship and chant had filled it with a kind of holy illumination, I listened, opening my own inner space to respond. There were no sounds, not even of birdsong outside. Nothing to distract or divert my attention. The place was full of reflected light. The interior silence and solitude felt like liberation rather than suffocation. The words that came to me, inaudible but real, and repeated, were, "Continue to be faithful, *not knowing*."

It was the same message I'd heard many years before, over and over again, during the dark months of my first husband Harold's terminal lung cancer and dying as I wondered why this great and good man was being lifted away in the prime of his life. Leaving me with a publishing house to run and a teenage daughter deprived of her father at a critical age. As I felt doubts about God's goodness rising in me like methane bubbles from a swamp, I remember writing down in my journal this advice from the medieval mystic who wrote about overcoming the dread of not knowing: "Strike upon the cloud of unknowing with the sharp dart of longing love. Come what may, never give up."[6]

And after Harold's funeral I wondered, *But how is such persistence, such consistency possible over a lifetime?* The frustration of it! I'd sometimes wondered if my very longing for God was a kind of magnet, drawing me toward him. But he seemed infinities-of-time-and-space distant from me. There had been some answers to my prayer, a few gleams of truth and trust, but they didn't last, and I was left hanging on to a batch of Bible promises about God's faithfulness. That which I seek, *him* whom I seek, seemed unknowable in the mystery of transcendence. Jesus lived two thousand years ago. I wanted to touch him, like the woman in the Gospels with a history of inadequate medical help. Though we are given gleams and glances of light, of perception, sudden epiphanies when everything hangs together and makes sense, they are so often withdrawn, capriciously it sometimes seems.

The Hebrew Scriptures use the word *yada*, "knowing," to describe sexual congress. "[Adam] *knew* his wife Eve, and she conceived" (Genesis 4:1). That kind of intimate knowing, the entering of one body and soul by another, is what human beings are designed to desire. And to expect fruit, the birth of something new and unique, as a result. I wanted to know and believe in God in that intimate way. I wanted the indication of belief to incarnate itself in me so that the fruit of that union would be God-fruit.

The morning after settling in to my small living space with its vast view of the ocean, I woke early, in the cool before dawn. I was lying on my back, spread-eagled under a woolen blanket on the narrow bed, acutely aware of my lack, my longing. Awake and waiting. Was I praying? Not in any articulated way, but simply acknowledging how small and empty I felt. Later, in this poem, I recalled what happened:

On Retreat, New Camaldoli Hermitage, Big Sur

This early morning, in the chill before light,
I lie open, face upward on the narrow bed,
supplicant, body reflecting soul, ready
for something I cannot see, but crave.
At this height, I am already closer to heaven.

I'm waiting, like any bud in a garden,
to be rained on, or sun-drenched.

Oh, I am little, little.

The day lifts its face over the crest
and a corner of sun touches the thin pillow.
I shift my head under its warm hand;
it moves across my face as I lie quite still,
blinding me as it blesses my forehead
with its holy oil.

What is blessing but a largeness
so immense it crowds out
everything but itself?

I suppose I could've been cynical, thinking, *okay, the sun rises and sets regularly without any special, personal trigger from me or God*. But because I was listening and open, I acknowledged that a patch of morning sunlight, bright and warm as gold on my skin, felt like a gentle invasion, a divine marking, an anointing. It was as if God was laying his hand on my forehead, assuring me, "Oh yes. I really am here with you. You needed and I provided. I'm welcoming you into my presence. It's my love that is entering you."

My journal was at hand. I sat up on my cot and reached for my pen. The arrival of the poem itself, an extra gift coming at this moment of revelation, was part of God's answer to my neediness. Often that is how I know the Spirit is at work, when a poem dances into my mind in response to a fresh insight. Sometimes the poem comes first and leads me into a perception that my rational mind has not yet discovered. I am made to be printed with words and the realities they speak of. It takes practice to develop such an awareness, and I'd devoted much of my life to being open to sudden insights. This is a large part of creativity—the openness to wisdom from beyond me.

Relationship with the Creator is like a dance—an entreaty, a response, a joining, a celebration. Years earlier, in a time of similar urgent spiritual emptiness, stopping my car and pulling over to the side of a California back road I opened the window.

For an hour or two my little Civic became for me a temple of the Holy Ghost. That time I had parked roadside in the center of a stand of tall eucalyptus trees whose pungent fragrance filled the car like incense.

The Blue Eyeball

The grove, and this huge eucalyptus tree
leaning over me. In the clasp of two
saber-shaped leaves heaven looked like
the gaze of God peering through the eye of a needle.
The sky's air — intense as a rare bead of clear
cobalt sea-glass — God looked straight through,
through me, as though my transparency
were something he craved.

And then, rising from stillness, the air
began breathing, began rearranging
the leaves. Oh, they closed — God's eyelids.
Clouds arrived in their dark boats over
the waves of hills. My view of heaven
was shut. But then, in a thin wire
of lightning, he spoke into me the promise —
his view of me will not be held back
by clouds, two leaves, a forest.

"There is certainly nothing so obscure or contemptible in which some marks of the power and wisdom of God may not be seen," said John Calvin.[7] I look for signs. I take them in like necessary food. I check them against known wisdom, but always watch for evidence of God's print on my surroundings and in my soul—fingerprints, markings to identify me with the Printmaker and point me back to him.

Such revelations arrive at moments of need and felt inadequacy, blessing me, as encouraging as a friend holding my hand, helping me up a steep path.

Oh, I wish that all of us yearning seekers can be ready, opening ourselves continually to this oneness of light and love. Soaking it in, allowing us to be illuminated so that we will return our joy and love to the Creator at the heart of the universe!

four

The Markings of Grace

*I*f we are pragmatists, the kind of people who simply want things to work with relative efficiency and who plan their lives around that strategy; if as human beings we seem unable to be a bit awed and amazed about the wonder workings of the world, it might seem enough to live in a *functional* universe, with self-sustaining life forms that replicate themselves and keep the world going and growing. For the Designer and Architect of our planet to add beauty to the mix and to supply us women and men with an aesthetic sense that compels us to respond to what is beautiful, as well as to celebrate it, is a blessing. Added to that, if we also have the ability to *originate* things of beauty, it seems to be an act of pure grace. In the truest and most positive sense of the word, it is *gratuitous*.

Unearned, deeply desired.

The Benedictines have long held that beauty is "truth shining into being," a principle echoed by John Keats in his famous line "Beauty is truth, truth beauty."[1] In a sense beauty is redemptive. Generous. It can lift our spirits, inspiring us (and the word *inspired* really means "in-spirited," being breathed into and invigorated by God's Spirit). It can even motivate us to turn a corner, to pursue a new objective, to make a decisive choice. It awakens in us a fresh awareness because it is often surprising enough to startle, showing up in unexpected forms and places.

C. S. Lewis found that beauty could summon in him a sudden, surprising joy, a hint of what we might expect in heaven. One of his poems is titled "The Day with a White Mark," in which he affirmed that even the most ordinary of objects and events seemed to lift his spirits and renew his hope, while adverse things had no power to dampen his day.[2] Lewis referred to such moments as "patches of God-light," like glimmers of sunlight in a dark wood. Os Guinness has called them "gleams of transcendence."

Beauty was one of the three Platonic ideals—companion of Truth and Goodness. For Plato, being human meant having to recognize and endeavor to embody these ideals. Beauty itself is no abstraction; it is always tied to the real, the observable. It is there to be seen, felt, heard, experienced. I even find it in the morning moments I spend drinking that dark, pungent coffee from one of my (insanely beautiful) mugs.

The Christian church has given considerable attention to Truth and Goodness, to theology and ethics, doctrine and morality. But in spite of all the centuries of holy art, too often Beauty, or an appreciation of the aesthetic, has escaped Christian believers, or we have attempted to evade or devalue it. Perhaps this is partly because of creativity's innovative, experimental aspect, its way of reaching for originality, or an untried way of expressing a value or truth. Many church-going, conservative Christians have viewed this exploratory element in art as perilous because it allows the imagination of flawed and fallen humankind to run free and perhaps stray too far from God-given truth. The fact that God himself is a fountain of beauty (some would say "herself" or, as Madeleine L'Engle would say, "El-self," speaking of a deity too large to be limited by gender) has been ignored. Thank God, this attitude is changing. Communities that gather around the relationship between faith and art are making us aware of new possibilities and opening new avenues for the expression of the beautiful as a way of glorifying God. Artists in many mediums are working out of their divinely given insights, translating their spiritual visions into visual or expressive forms.

The pursuit of beauty has been seen as a somewhat controversial or frivolous option, and an undomesticated one at that, because beauty can neither be controlled nor programmed. As Eugene Peterson has said, "[Beauty] works out of the unconscious, is not practical, cannot be quantified, is not efficient, and cannot be 'used' for very long without corrupting either the art or the artist."[3]

In the unpretentious chapel where my family and I worshiped early in my life, the pews were hard, the architecture blocky, utilitarian. The minimal allowances for the aesthetic were the windows—large frosted panes of pink, white and yellow; this pastel glass was permitted to illuminate us, but there was no cross or other ornamentation in the Gospel Hall (it was never called the church or the sanctuary) except for a verse of Scripture painted across the front wall—"Gathered in His Name." It was implied that we all knew who "He" was— the center of our worship. The stated attempt was to worship together in "the simplicity of Christ." The fact that my great-great-grandfather had been one of the original founders to shape this movement made it feel especially sacrilegious for me to critique or diverge from it.

I believe in the value of simplicity, a drawing down to essentials, a recognition of what is fundamental and indispensable. Its value lies in its focus, boldness and purity. It makes an uncompromising statement. But another part of me hungers for diversity, for multiplicity, for the splendor of light seen through a prism in all its colors. Madeleine L'Engle once gave me a faceted crystal ball that still hangs from a nylon thread in my office window. Through it an arm of sun can dapple all the walls with rainbow color, moving across the room as the sun arcs across the sky. It's a sign, a symbol of the multiplicity of beauty and the power of light to transform.

I've come to believe that a hunger for beauty as a reflection of God is implicit in the human spirit. It shows up in the pictures on our walls, the color scheme in our living rooms, the arrangement of our furniture, the patterns on our dishes and the landscaping in our gardens. None of these is vital for bodily survival. Yet the urge toward design and ornamentation persists. In the Plymouth Brethren church of my childhood, though a piano—known as the "wooden brother"—was not to be used except to accompany Sunday school songs, doctrinal truths and the words of Scripture were set to music for worship, and the hymns, many composed by my great-great-grandfather, were sung a cappella and beautifully harmonized. (As a result, it became second nature for me to sing the alto part in any hymn, in any church setting.) In that humble chapel we were stumbling toward musical beauty without ever acknowledging its appeal.

"Beauty will save the world," proclaimed Fyodor Dostoyevsky, as if God's primary device for healing and restoration is an appreciation of the beautiful, the wholeness of beauty. And now, Dostoyevsky, by way of *Image*, the premier journal of art, faith and mystery, has generously supplied the bumper sticker on my car, alerting people in the vehicles behind me on the highway to this large statement that embraces every aspect of grace.

For most of us the messages of beauty through the senses, when combined with the responses of our reasoning intelligence, achieve meaning or significance. These messages are caught, snagged, hooked into our minds and memories.

The music of Bach sings in my brain. And the great orchestral compositions of Brahms. And Fauré. And Rutter.

And Stravinsky. And Rachmaninoff. And of course, the "Hallelujah Chorus." The national anthem, as well as "Yankee Doodle"! I sing in our church choir, which means that I have the alto part of many great anthems memorized; I can hear them in my ear. (I have to admit my voice sounds better to me when joined with the other parts!)

Then there are the visual arts. I was thrilled last month to visit the Rijksmuseum in Amsterdam. Familiar already (mentally imprinted) with many reproductions of Rembrandt's and Vermeer's paintings, I was thrilled anew to view the originals up close in all their power. Now they have made their fresh mark on me. I have many artist friends whose work is shown in galleries and public spaces. I met with them recently at a gathering of Christians in the Visual Arts, a group of dedicated artists whose mandate is to celebrate their faith and calling to the arts. My granddaughter Lauren, who teaches printmaking at a major university, has painted huge murals in airports. She sometimes turns paper into smaller works of art, using wax, a sharp knife, a sewing machine to craft multi-colored shapes and assemblages. In her work the ordinary becomes extraordinary.

I have an extensive library—poetry, fiction, critique and commentary—and even though I've promised myself to buy no more books, they keep showing up! The words and concepts of great writings—so many I can't list them all—have left their impressions like pictures on the film of my imaginations, and continue to do their transforming work in me, reminding me, if I am aware, of the One who is the Word behind the messages. And for me those messages translate into ongoing, penetrating Love. Not anything sentimental, but strong, enduring, overcoming. Powerful.

Though each of us has an intensely personal idea of what is beautiful, experienced moment by moment in individuals with vastly differing tastes and standards, the appeal of beauty seems universal. All of us on the planet may be transfixed at the sight of breakers sending up violent white curtains of foam as they crash on the coastal rocks. Frozen waterfalls and ice caves. Hillsides decorated with tablecloths of wild flowers. Unless we are beset with allergies, we breathe in the delicious smell of a newly cut hayfield, with its moist fragrances.

A Celebration of Weeds

I don't think the way you think. . . . As rain falls and waters the earth, doing the work of making things grow and producing seed, so will my words work. Is. 55:8, 10

For I am considering, before I grow very old, too old
to drive, how gloriously the grasses ornament the road's
verges, its ditches, flowing then across the fields, waves
of green, meadows that dance to the fists of wind. Weeds,
all and every, long and lovely and lush (Hopkins' language
rings wild on the ear). Sheep crop, cool in oak shade.
All feral stems, each a primary act of God, sing the hymns

of air, his persistent garden in spite of our ravaging machines
resilient, needing no fertilizer to flourish.

The car snakes along the dirt road—a necessary scar on
the body of earth—and now I consider yarrow, how its
white, starred bed sheet is draped over this next meadow.
And now, a low kindling of fire-weed purples through the windshield,
nothing I haven't seen before, but in this moment, extraordinary.

I am tuned to the communities of herbs growing, to a haze
of salt hay decorated with grasshoppers, those pale jade
phenomena that leap continually in God's imagination—
or brambles and thrusting blackberries, their glowing fruit
there for the taking, their juice an extract of rain.
How his spirit animates all blades and glades with pure daylight!
How his stalks gesture and bow, saluting their own faces in
the clear stream that flows under the bridge! Clovers' trinity leaves.
Buds, bursting into their particular selves, all then
melted by vision into a fusion from this generous confusion.
And the dandelions, small sunbursts on every bank, wanton
and innocent, without evil intent, uncanny in their abundance
in noon light, feeling no need to justify their existence.

And tonight, in the dark, I will remember how flower heads
fold into themselves, stems lengthen, rising after rain, or
seeded by stars and a moon as yellow as a midday
buttercup. And it is all good. All good. God said it.

A close, loving friend recently sent me, in a birthday gift package, an assortment of small tokens that speak to each of my senses: lavender soap for smell, three brass bells for hearing, chocolate toffee for taste, lotion for touch, a refrigerator magnet with a photo for vision. Their beauty lies not in the items themselves, endearing as they are, but in the thoughtfulness that had assembled, gift-wrapped and mailed them to me.

That is beauty close at hand, warming, diminutive, intimate. But think about the larger dimension of our being—how awed we are, standing under the spaciousness of the night sky, seeded with far stars. This happens only when we are distant enough from a city to be undistracted by ambient light.

Living in most any modern town it is hard to see the glory of the night heavens clearly. After sundown, all around us are the street and traffic lights, searchlights from the nearby airport and the moving headlights of cars. To find space and quiet to think and just be, I often go to Laity Lodge, a campground and retreat center in the hill country of Texas. It is so remote that after traveling west for hours along long highways from San Antonio, guests have to enter the property and drive half a mile along the Frio riverbed to get to the lodge. For several years Madeleine L'Engle and I were there for a week at a time, leading groups of creative writers.

One evening at Laity, when the busy day of teaching and writing sessions was over, we were free to walk together in the

dark up the dirt road to the top of a bluff, the perfect spot to
see the night sky. We turned off our flashlights and just stood
there, breathless. A cool night, with no wind, felt fresh on our
faces. We could gaze up at what looked like a star map, a sky
absolutely infested with lights. We could see the difference
between the far and the near stars, as the three (or more) di-
mensions of bodies in space were highlighted by the darkness
around them, and around us. That expansive experience of the
universe drew us both into the embrace of the Creator God of
the universe. A universal Beauty! (Years earlier Madeleine had
taken me to her own "star-gazing rock" near her home back
in the hills of Goshen, Connecticut, far from the lights of a
town, to experience the immensity of the night sky.)

Along our Northwest coast, night fog often creeps in from
the ocean, laying its filmy blanket over Bellingham Bay, the
town, the foothills. When the fog lifts, we are transfixed at the
sight of the peak of our snow-covered Mount Baker (always
there, like God, but sometimes unseen in the mists). Close up
we marvel at the glory of its glaciers and the brilliant, ethereal
blue of light leaking through ice. More beauty.

Or we call out to our spouse to come and witness with us
a double rainbow over the lake, or the golden glory of the sun
setting behind spectacular purple clouds (I did this just the
other night).

Around the planet the striking earth tones of the Kalahari,
the Sahara, the Himalayan range and Ayers Rock call us to

wonder and worship, along with the painted deserts and canyons of Utah and Arizona and New Mexico. The mighty roar of a Niagara. The great evergreen forests of the northern wilderness. The vastness of the Gobi. The verdant rainforests in the South Island of New Zealand.

It's something to experience this beauty firsthand. But even greater, an appreciation of all this loveliness keeps bursting out in the arts and has been captured and translated graphically by artists throughout history and around the globe.

In our travels we've noticed the creative soul work that goes into the planning and building of sacred spaces. Hundreds of years of planning and construction (and immense wealth) go into the construction of cathedrals and abbeys and smaller houses of worship, some sacred spaces magnificent, some less conspicuous. I've entered and been overwhelmed by the richly ornamented Cathedral of San Marco in Venice. And Coventry Cathedral, still showing the marks of wartime destruction. And Cologne Cathedral rising above the banks of the Rhine. The massive Cathedral of St. John the Divine in Manhattan, to which Madeleine L'Engle and I would often walk for noon prayer. I've preached in Christ Church Cathedral in Victoria, British Columbia. Mentally I contrast all these awesome, enormous spaces with a small enclosure carved out of a precipitous rock face in southern France, with one luminous, round, blue glass window depicting a moon surrounded by stars. The whole universe seemed to be

probing that small space and flowing out of it. Sacred beauty
gleams from the large and the small.

We recently built and moved into a new house, less spacious
and more efficient than the home we'd lived in for fifteen
years, this new dwelling designed to be well suited to our later
years. Robin, my oldest daughter, is an interior designer, and
together we explored the multiple options for floor coverings,
countertops, colored bathroom tiles, and the tonal varieties
for wood cabinets and storage spaces. Once it was built, we
brought over from the old house the rugs and carpets that I'd
collected over the years—from Turkey, India and New Mexico,
and the large living room rug in deep pinks and greens and
blues that I'd bought many years ago (with poetry royalties!)
from Marshall Field's in Chicago. Even the windows, inten-
tionally without drapes, allow us the view of Bellingham Bay,
its light gleaming up at us from below.

In our living room we have a large Indian brass tray from
my parents' early married lives, incised with decorative pat-
terns and repeatedly polished with Brasso so it shines like the
sun. It is centered on an intricately carved wooden stand, also
from India. I not only love these pieces themselves and the
reminders of my parents' choices, but applaud the craftspeople
who brought them into being, following their own styles of
cultural beauty.

On our walls we've hung contemporary paintings by
some of my artist friends like Ed Knippers, Erica Grimm,

Norah Beaumont, Ken Smith and my granddaughter Lauren, as well as a series of Barry Moser wood engravings of "winged creatures" (angels, a stork, a hawk, a raven). I have a small, brilliant icon of *Madonna and Child* in silver, gold and porcelain, a birthday present from my prayer friend Bev Gorsuch. I mention these items to show off not any great wealth but the diversities of beauty and generosity that reveal to me aspects of grace.

And then there's the landscape of the earth itself in its un-selfconscious glory:

Tenting, Burr Trail, Long Canyon, Escalante

Even when I close my eyes, even later in
the tent, dreaming, I see banks and rivers running red.
My blood has drunk color from the stones as if
it were the meal I needed. I am ready to eat
any beauty — these vistas of stars, storms.
The mesas and vermillion cliffs. The light they magnify
into the canyon. The echoes, the distances.
The rocks carved with ancient knowledge.

But after vast valleys, I am so ready for this
low notch in the gorge, the intimate cottonwoods
lifting their leafy skirts and blowing their small
soft kisses into my tent on the wasteland's
stringy breath. The spaces between the gusts are rich

with silence. I am ready to stay in this one place, sleep,
dream, breathe the grace of wind and earth that is
never too much, and more than I will ever need.

In this parchment land, the scribble
and blot of junipers and sagebrush, each crouched
separate, rooted in its own desert space,
spreads low to the sand, holding it down
the way the tent-pegs anchor my tent, keep it
from blowing away. The way I want my words
to hold, growing maybe an inch a year,
grateful for the least glisten of dew.

I want the stamp, the impression of my words, to last, to
gesture to something that has leaped into significance for me,
so that I can point it out to you and believe that you will see
it too. I long for you to share my wonder and respond. I want
to strike a metaphorical match and light your candle. I hope
and pray that an image or a fresh idea has been powerful
enough to become a part of you, imprinting you and ex-
panding your own awareness. I am just one of a long line of
creatures whose mandate is to create, in the image of a Creator.

When I say I want the stamp, the imprint of my life, to last,
I'm voicing a universal, primordial human need. I'm saying, I
don't want to be snuffed out like a lamp—everything I've
thought and said and done lost to thin air and utterly for-
gotten, after a meaningless life. Somehow, you and I need to

know that we've made a difference. That we've added to our environment a tiny pebble or color or fiber, some word of truth, some act of compassion, some appreciation that adds to the sum total of what God was after when he created sentient, intelligent human beings who are capable of response to the planet we live on, and its inhabitants.

Jesus, with the destiny of the whole world hanging on his death and resurrection, not wanting his sacrifice to be obliterated by centuries, voiced this essential principle about our participation in his body and blood: "Do *this* to remember me." And as we do it, as we eat and drink of the essential elements that sustain life—food and drink, wine and wafer—we are enacting and re-enacting the profound metaphor of Christ's own creative self-sacrifice and self-giving. We are re-membering, with our bodies and our senses, so that the meaning of the incarnation is not lost, and so that we can participate and not forget.

The faithful prophet Nehemiah asked of Yahweh, "Remember me, O my God, for this. Don't ever forget the devoted work I have done" (Nehemiah 13:14 *The Message*). My good friend Barry Moser, the great and gifted engraver and illustrator who set in type the entire King James Version of the Bible (the Pennyroyal Caxton edition), enhancing it with numerous striking woodcuts of biblical characters and events, refuses to sign his name on this unique work of art and literature, preferring to reference Nehemiah's plea for remembrance as his own penciled, barely visible autograph. It's as if he is saying, "Remember, I did this to honor God's work and words, not my own skill."

This kind of remembering, this place-holding technique, goes back to the time of the patriarchs. Yahweh told his people not to forget his laws: "Keep these words that I am commanding you today in your heart. Recite them to your children and talk about them when you are at home and when you are away, when you lie down and when you rise. Bind them as a sign on your hand, fix them as an emblem on your forehead, and write them on the doorposts of your house and on your gates" (Deuteronomy 6:6-9). In other words, you Israelis, I'm imprinting you with my standards for holiness; everything about your life should be a witness that you are God's special people. And don't you ever forget it!

Crunching Jesus

John 6:53-58

The communion bread is laid on my tongue
so gently. But I am ravenous; I want to gnaw
the whole loaf. We know already we are his body,
but taking in this crumb of the earth's generous
flesh, this sip of its given blood, presses Incarnation

into our flesh. By way of imagination we take in
the symbol and the substance to become
more vividly vessels filled with Christ, so that
even as we step away from the altar and out
the church door we keep living the liturgy and the urge
to Eat and Drink. The wine burns still in my throat.
I have a shred of bread stuck in my teeth. Oh, how
to feed the hunger and thirst of the world?

Oh, how to invigorate the world with remembrance! How to make the imprint visible!

five

Determining Identity

$\mathcal{A}$s for impressions and imprints, I have a confession to make. I'm a bit of an addict of TV shows like *CSI* and *Law & Order* and *Blue Bloods* and other criminal investigation entertainments, in which forensic inquiries play a large part in determining and tracking down the perpetrator of a crime. DNA and fingerprints provide evidence that is often conclusive in bringing the perpetrator to justice because it is universally believed that no two humans have exactly the same configurations of grooves and ridges on their fingers or toes. Similarly, our chromosomes—the sequences of genes in our ribonucleic acid—are specific within each individual.

It's all a testimony to human uniqueness; if the print of *A* is on the gun, *B* could not have committed the crime. If *C*'s prints show up on the car door handle, maybe *D* can be exonerated. A shred of skin under a fingernail may be examined for DNA and matched with its corresponding constituent from a mouth swab or the smear of saliva on the lip of a wine glass. It's a kind of sorting mechanism, a way of determining identity within a complex set of circumstances and possibilities. The fact that the detectives can access a database of the digital prints and DNA samples of former criminals, along with facial recognition programs, adds to the speed and efficiency of the system in preventing or tracking down further criminal activity.

Last year a friend added to my understanding of a thumbprint's significance. He had seen an exhibit of Leonardo da Vinci's work at the Art Institute in Chicago and told me something he'd learned: "Leonardo didn't always sign his pieces; sometimes he left his thumbprint in the paint before it dried. For some of his works it was the only proof of their authenticity. No other artist's thumbprint would do." And to add to the evidence, Leonardo was left-handed.

In the *New Yorker* I read a lengthy article about the authentication of works of art, which is "an often bitterly contested skill."[1] Of Martin Kemp, professor emeritus of art history at Oxford University and an expert on the life and work of Leonardo, the author writes, "When vetting a painting he proceeds methodically, analyzing brush-strokes, composition, iconography, and pigments—those elements which may reveal an artist's hidden identity."[2] An undisputed Leonardo painting of St. Jerome that hangs in the Vatican shows one of his clearest fingerprints.

Of course, the paintings of Leonardo and other Renaissance artists are now sold for such magnificent sums of money that skilled forgeries have become more commercially seductive. Experts hunt for clues to such fakes in the kind of pigments used, the direction of the brush strokes, and so on, because "every painter has his own peculiarities that escape him without his being aware."[3]

Canadian forensic art expert Peter Paul Biro scours paintings for the artist's fingerprints impressed either on the paint, the canvas or its frame. Sometimes an artist will even have used the palm of his hand to soften the shading within the painting, leaving an incontrovertible evidence of authorship. J. M. W. Turner, the great English landscape painter, would actually work with his fingertips to model the paint on the canvas. Experts claim to have found hundreds of such tiny swirls in Turner's paintings—loops, whorls and tented arches, those unique confirmations of the artist's identity. However, many prints are too partial or too indistinct for final proof. The *New Yorker* article concludes that not every scientific authenticator agrees with Kemp or Biro. This is an area where experts differ, and much further research needs to be done.

The intricacy and individuality of digital whorls and ridges on our fingers and thumbs is only one instance of the complexity and infinite variety of creation. The word *digit* is interesting. It essentially means *one*, or a single number in the series one through nine. The word comes from the Latin for "finger" or "toe," of which all primates have five on each of their extremities. The Egyptian cubit was divided into twenty-eight portions, each the breadth of a finger, or two centimeters. In modern technology the designation *digital* refers to the rapid transfer of information by means of a binary code—a series of combinations of zeroes and ones—rather than an analog.

Braille is the language developed for the blind that conveys information through touch rather than sight by means of a system of raised dots on paper or signboards; I've seen them by elevators and in public restrooms. With practice, a blind person's fingertips grow extraordinarily sensitive to such delicate but powerful stimuli. My husband purchased a copy of the Episcopal *Book of Common Prayer* in Braille for a blind friend to use during the worship at our church. It enabled her to participate more fully with the congregation than if she relied entirely on her hearing to know where the liturgy was leading and what responses were appropriate.

There is some anguish these days in the literary community about the future of printed books. Some of the largest bookstore chains are closing, squeezed out of the book-selling business by the growing popularity and availability of digitized ebooks on Kindle, Nook, iPad and similar devices, and the easy downloading of books available on the Internet.

Some readers, including me, feel the loss of the sensual pleasures associated with opening the covers of a colorful, beautifully bound book with a well-designed dust jacket and end papers, feeling the fine paper with the fingers, noticing the book design—art in the hand—admiring the photo of the author, the motif or font used for the chapter headings, the placement of page numbers, the readable typeface, even smelling the printer's ink with its faint, distinctive aroma. For many of us, opening such a book is a supreme delight that launches us on a journey of exploration. An adventure awaits as we move ahead into someone else's vision and discovery, turning the pages with heightened expectation. I'm waiting, but not hoping, to be convinced that digital books may yield similar pleasures.

We associate this delight with a lifetime of reading and learning from the printed page. A book that we can take physically from its companions on a bookshelf in a library is a friend we can count on to lift us away from ourselves or to print itself and its content on our memories and imaginations. Manually turning a page is both a tactile and an emotional experience. Somehow touching a button on a glass surface or the metal rim of a digital reader fails to satisfy those of us whose delight has been to progress through a "page turner" with the astonished excitement of anticipation as a plot or a line of thought unfolds and resolves with a sigh on the final page, like a wave dying on a beach. (Disclaimer:

I now have an iPad, a birthday gift. I need to learn to love it!) Culture and its habits continually shift and reconfigure. As we adapt to the new technologies, we may find they have their own challenges and delights. I sometimes find black words on white backgrounds dancing in my head after closing a book or shutting down my computer screen. The visual imprints swim for a while on the inside of my eyelids like emoticons.

That is one level of change that we feel urged by the industry to adjust to. Ereaders are the new repositories of so much information in one easy-to-carry device that seem to make a shelf of books in a library redundant. We can take our clever new contraption to read novels or poetry or listen to music on the plane as we fly to a vacation resort. We can take it to our beach chair along with our drink, dark glasses and suntan lotion. It has become a kind of fashion accessory that frees us from burden bearing. Unlimited resources and delight are accessible without effort. There are no library expiration dates to worry about.

This is all a part of the escalating race toward the convenience and technological advance that characterizes our culture. Very soon new and even more extraordinary techniques will make the present ones obsolete. Human beings appear to be becoming more robotized. Call me a holdout, a Luddite, but I wonder whether the great stores of ancient wisdom are easily amenable to such reduction.

This is one area of concern. Okay, we rightly worry about how many trees it takes to make the paper in a printed volume, and perhaps reducing information to words on a screen protects the forests. At a more primal level there seem to be warnings about the kind of abstraction that digitized information presents. I have a download of the Bible on my smartphone, and that may be helpful to reference a phrase or passage of Scripture or to check on the wording of a particular verse. But that is not how I can meditatively dwell in what God is saying to me.

For remember, the Word became flesh. Bones. Blood. God's message was so utterly embodied in a human being that the apostle John could describe Jesus as one "which we have heard, which we have seen with our eyes, which . . . our hands have handled" (1 John 1:1 KJV). Here is the kind of enfleshed, palpable Truth that resists being reduced to a mechanical device.

My bookseller friend Warren Farha of Eighth Day Books in Wichita (some of us call him St. Warren) is convinced that books made of paper and ink are as sacramentally important as the bodily realities of human beings. And it is in the flesh of a human being that God made himself available to us, linking the biological *us* with the transcendent. I once asked my rector what image came immediately to his mind when I mentioned the word *incarnation*. His instant response: "meat." It is not an accident that Jesus, that bodily showing of God, is called the Word, as if truth is issuing from some immortal mouth. The words in books come to me as little incarnations, thoughts and ideas become flesh.

I realize that culture and its habits continually change. As we adapt to the new technologies, we may find they have their own challenges and delights.

Nevertheless the discoveries and applications of science and physics expand exponentially as the boundaries of knowledge are pushed further and further back (should we say *forward*?) and deeper and deeper in. With the discovery in the last century of phenomena such as the double helix, molecules and quasars and quarks, quantum physics, string theory, burgeoning astrophysics, the patterns of genes and chromosomes, and the completed genome mapping project, physics and metaphysics seem to merge to give us clues to the way the world is and who we are. The actuality of the Higgs boson (sometimes called "The God Particle") intuited by Peter Higgs in the last century and now revealed by the Large Hadron Collider (CERN), the powerful particle accelerator, opens up enormous possibilities. Some scientists are persuaded that these phenomena demonstrate more than just *physical* evidence of complexity. More and more they have begun to imply meaning and purpose, and as we open to such intangibles the more we can hope to see. They have significance beyond themselves. They become personal in the reality they assume in our intelligence.

If we are rational enough to believe in cause and effect, and as we notice that human beings universally respond to beauty in its multiform array, we have to trust that the two are related. A meaningless universe would require no such connection. And yet the human quest for meaning is evident throughout all times and civilizations, as evidenced in the forms and forays of human worship and sense of the transcendent—that there is something splendidly significant beyond us yet surrounding us, often veiled in mystery, beyond human knowing, though we long always to know it. And that longing imprints the trajectories of our lives. It pushes me to pursue, to keep seeking, to ask questions and not be satisfied until the magnificent responses arrived and continue to arrive.

There is an altarpiece by the nineteenth-century artist Gustavus Johann Grunewald in the Eisenheim Chapel in Alsace that shows Jesus on the cross. To his left, John the apostle is seen pointing his elongated forefinger at the dying Christ as if to say, "Look! *This* is the Savior of the world." It is fascinating to me that in this painting of the crucified Jesus, Grunewald highlighted the spots on Christ's skin—pitted with plague-type sores—with which the ailing, disease-ridden people of the time could identify. Yet between John's pale, pointing finger and the figure on the cross is a dark distance that seems to indicate to human beings, "This is a mystery." How authentically can the truest, most perceptive human witness proclaim the truth?

Pierre Teilhard de Chardin, a Jesuit priest (but also an internationally respected paleontologist, philosopher and traveler who explored widely in Asia), became convinced that the church's teachings on human origins and significance were flawed. In his extended essay "*The Future of Man*" (1950), he posited what he called "the Omega Point," the ultimate state of complexity and consciousness toward which the created universe and its inhabitants are moving as they evolve. And the conclusion he drew was that the divine imperative for human beings was to be found in Christ, the Logos, who "draws all things unto himself," according to the words of the Nicene Creed, and that "through him all things were made." (It should be noted that not all theologians or theoreticians agreed with de Chardin's theory, viewing it as overly mechanistic.)

A favorite quote of mine from Annie Dillard (she wrote it when *Life* magazine asked her for her definition of the meaning of life) goes like this: "We are here to abet Creation and to witness it, to notice each thing so each thing gets noticed. Together we notice not only each Mountain shadow and each stone on the beach, but we notice each other's beautiful face and complex nature so that Creation need not play to an empty house."

Another responder to the world we live in, poet Mary Oliver, says,

If you notice anything
it leads you to notice
more
and more.[4]

In this and the last century's fascination with spirituality (however that elastic term may have been defined or abused), we have begun again to probe our longings for faith formation and spiritual mentoring. How do I know the most ideal way forward for my life? What is it that informs my choices and decisions?

This is an urgent area of need for any of us who live with an open mind to hearing and following the purposes of God in our personal lives. How am I meant to determine forward movement? Say three doors of opportunity have opened for me. Which to do I enter? Or, if every door seems to be closed, do I batter them down one by one, or do I seek another direction?

When Solomon prayed for "an understanding mind," he wanted what may be translated as "a listening heart." This is a crucial way to begin discernment—to hear guidance both from within ourselves and from beyond ourselves. Listening is a divine art. And it's hard to listen attentively with all the background clatter that accompanies contemporary living. There's an urgent need for us to take time for silence, for solitude, for meditation, for discerning discussions within our close communities. Fr. Richard Keating's emphasis on the practice of "centering prayer" is a case in point.[5]

I love the word *vocation*. It makes me think of God vocalizing in my direction a song that suggests that I am being called, that I have a voice to listen to, an ear to hear and a direction, a new trajectory, that beckons me to travel. This may involve developing an already active spiritual gift or natural ability. I may be hopeless at algebra but have a sensitivity to words and pictures and the way they work to enrich our human thinking and spread our insights beyond ourselves. Our natural gifts are not there for nothing.

It's true that our experience or giftedness may point to a specific path, but what if God wants to steer us off the beaten path, suggesting something entirely new for us? It's disheartening simply to list my own preferences; they all seem so self-serving. In my church the practice of discernment is a community activity. If someone in our church family senses a vocation that suggests a move in a new direction or taking up a new role, time is taken within a discernment group in which each listens to others' stories and inclinations, others' gifts and experience, so that in prayer a future path may become more distinct. Then it's the group's responsibility to follow up with a commitment to continuing support and prayer.

Moving on from the earlier context of crime detection, I've wondered about what I might call the forensics of spiritual discernment. *Forensics* is the scientific term used to ascertain the facts after the fact. The word comes from the ancient practice of showing evidence before a Greek forum whose task it was to determine who, after a crime was committed, was responsible for a misdeed and how. In the ancient world such forums often relied on forced confessions and corrupted witness testimony. This accounted for many wrong convictions of the innocent. The awkward word *disambiguation* is a synonym for *forensics* and describes the process of discovering what is or is not certain. Though no one wants ambiguity in separating right from wrong, clear-cut evidence isn't always easy to come by.

So, what tools may we use to discern the direction of our life's forward movement? Do we have some spiritual GPS that not only shows the best route to a destination for a fruitful life but informs us, in a no-nonsense voice, when we've taken the wrong turn, like the strident but knowledgeable woman behind the GPS on our car dashboard?

In my youth, the assumption among conservative Christians was that there was only one specific "divine will" for each one of us. And we had to seek that imperative no matter how difficult it was to know for sure. Since then we have had reason to question that narrow destination. Many of us, raised perhaps in an environment where faith was codified and ironclad, have had to move away from the dictates of that rigidity, ruled as it is by the fear of infringement and its penalties. It may have stamped us with anxiety that our earnest efforts are not enough; not the heavenly imprint we might have hoped for.

I went to Wheaton College bearing the urgent imprint of my missionary family, not just my parents but a whole generation of aunts and uncles and cousins who had felt the call to live and serve in foreign countries, learn difficult new languages and adopt cultures that must at first have seemed strange and alien. God's call on their lives was preeminent.

My parents' vision for me suggested a major in Christian education, or at least anthropology. The latter department had recently closed down, and instead I took some deadly dull courses in education. Until I needed to get a required literature course under my belt. And then I knew, *knew*, that I belonged in a discipline that focused on imagination and the words that bring it to life, with teachers who shared my passion for the English language. I prospered, came to life, felt gloriously at home in the English literature department and later was able to graduate with high honors.

How are we to interpret the light that we are given? What are the tools for the task?

I believe the first requirement is desire—a longing for clarity. It's a search that continues, that may last for a lifetime, much like the way a road winds over hills and down again but never comes to a dead end. Our passivity, our reluctance to take risks may well frustrate God's desire for us and deny his offer of guidance and preservation.

We may ask ourselves, What natural gifts or inclinations would fulfill my desire to live as God's faithful servant? Am I good with people, easily making friends and being faithful in friendships? Do I have a gift of stringing words together in a way that moves and stimulates those who listen to my speaking or read my writing? Do I have the kind of intellect that occupies itself with fresh, unconventional ideas that spur the thinking of others? Maybe I'm an entrepreneur with an original idea for a marketable product. Am I restless or contented? Am I easily swayed by the opinions of others for my life work?

When I was a young student entering college, my missionary parents longed for me to hear and answer the call to foreign missions. I wanted to please them, but the more I studied the clearer it became that the world of writing and literature was calling me to love words and language and learn to practice them.

But I have friends who have struggled for years to find themselves and their true calling. I love the oft-quoted advice from Frederick Buechner: "The place God calls you to is the place where your deep gladness and the world's deep hunger meet."[6] I long for those friends the sense of rightness that comes with that discovery.

Some of us have known nothing of deep worship but a form of glossy entertainment that in its reductionism ultimately fails to satisfy us (or, we've come to realize, God). Now we have the opportunity to question and explore. We have learned that it is possible to *doubt faithfully*.

I have come to believe that God is not at all bothered by our searching doubts and questionings. Just as we listen carefully and respond to our children's uncertainties and experimentations, grateful that they come to us for help, heavenly wisdom invites searching. Our souls expand during the exploration of new territory. Our struggles with the reality of faith prove the integrity of our search for truth, by which I mean our longing for the embodied, incarnated truth provided with such generosity by Jesus when he promised to send the Spirit of truth to lead us.

Still, there are times in the lives of many faithful people when we seem to find ourselves paralyzed in the heart of a black cloud of unknowing. The phrase described by St. John of the Cross—"the dark night of the soul"—has become almost a cliché, though when it happens it is so real that its particularity brings with it a sense of profound loneliness. Madeleine L'Engle talked of "a deep but dazzling darkness," a phrase used by metaphysical poet Henry Vaughn, in the midst of which, if we persist, God will show himself, leading us back to the very reason creation happened in the first place.

On Feeling Doubt

The trail of connections is frail. I listen
for the oblique to become transparent.

It feels like having to discover messages
in the silences between the calls

of the hoot owl on a moonless night.
Unmentioned images try to crowd

between the words on some page, leaving us
guessing. Conversation, the to

and fro of language, can never be a monolog.
I struggle for meaning, like angling my view for

the sparkles from a lump of coal ready
for burning, wondering about carbon—

its formation, its capacity for warming
a room, the life implicit in some Mesozoic tree.

I'm thinking of the hard questions we mortals find ourselves
asking if we dip below the surfaces of commonly accepted
truisms, the existential uncertainties that confront us as we
thoughtfully face life and mortality. We long to penetrate the
thick skin of reality. When a beloved friend or relative dies, we
ask: What just happened? Where did she go? Where is he now?
(And we wonder as well if they are conscious of our existence,
our grieving? How do we fully express our anguish? What
does *mortality* mean? How am I supposed to think about my
own inevitable aging and dying? And our joys? Are my an-
cestors thrilled that our child has found the love of his life?)

There are other questions, about life and its meaning, that haunt me. I didn't ask to be born, but here I am and what am I supposed to do about it? Is God truly personal enough to notice and respond to who I am and what I ask? And large enough, spatial enough to embrace me with all my questions? How can we learn to trust that which we cannot see, touch, hear, handle? That which confounds our rationality?

Such questions and explorations have needed an open avenue for expression. The sciences continue to push forward in dealing with the unknown. Brilliant and creative minds continue to batter the dense castle walls of our understanding of the universe, limited as it is. Scientists are explorers of mystery, though often it is the arts that have given us the opportunity to show that we have been created in the image of an imaginative Creator, and that imagination and imagery are ways of entering the mind of God, of approaching (though never completely comprehending) the mystery of the transcendent and the divine. And even the tools of science have their own beauty; a formula that works may be described as "elegant" in its simplicity and completeness!

Are we truth seekers? We must come to appreciate that truth is a lot larger than mere fact. In fact, the very word *truth* is an abstraction, referring to something too huge for any of us to encompass with our minds. *Truth* underlies *fact* the way the planet underlies the grain of sand on a beach. When Scripture encourages us "to seek and find" truth, or an aspect of truth, we need to trust the search. To seek and, in incremental and perhaps gradual and subtle ways, to find.

And keep on finding. Sometimes the discovery comes in a flash of insight; sometimes it comes with slow, patient thought and work and prayer, and by paying attention to the clues and hints provided along the way. We may find ourselves on a detour and, later, need to return to the originally appointed route. But if we don't get discouraged and give up, we will not remain stuck. The path will move forward before us, granting us incremental insights into who we are, who God is and why we are here in the first place.

six

Indelible Impressions

I've often found it helpful to penetrate the thicket of etymology and open up some definitions that seem to apply to the theme of being *marked*.

An *imprint* (noun and verb), or its variation, the Latin noun *imprimatur*, is used primarily to indicate the authorization of books or documents, to grant official endorsement. That was the whole idea behind the use of sealing wax, in which the unique emblem or imprint of an author or letter writer was pressed to "seal it," preserve it, and to show its attribution. The word *stamp* is a contemporary example—a bit of colored adhesive paper printed with a figure indicating its worth and an image identifying its country of origin, glued to a message to show that we have paid for the privilege of sending it through the Postal Service. Ancient coins were stamped with the likeness of an emperor or ruler to authenticate their value and emphasize where the authority to issue currency came from.

At the market I buy fruits and vegetable with stickers on them proclaiming their variety, and the identifying number assigned to them by the market system. Bananas, which our family consumes in vast quantities, bear the number 4011 along with a barcode. From the Golden Delicious apple I bit into today I had to peel away the sticker marked with the number 4021.

Sometimes I think I need a barcode myself, an identifying mark that allows me to feel distinct from all the multitudes on earth. I could paste it on my forehead as I go through the scanner! Of course, I count on the truth that God has already called and marked me, chosen and given me an identity different from any of his other creatively loved children.

The verb *stamp* also implies a physical demonstration of force and conviction. If I stamp my foot on the floor in anger or a fit of hysterical laughter, your attention is drawn to the sound and movement and you begin to understand that I'm feeling emphatic about something. At a football or basketball game, spectators, in their enthusiasm or frustration, may jump up and down, yell and clap their hands, stamping their emotions.

Impact, the noun, and the more recent verb *to impact*, both refer to what happens when we contact something firmly by pressure, or press it forcefully enough to make a change in its surface. Impact, and its intention, show up in the grooves, markings and patterns that a potter may inscribe on the surface of an artifact.

Impression and *impress*: Here's a similar word with varied uses. We talk about making a good first impression on a blind date (which is how I met my husband John, both of us widowed and introduced by mutual friends) or a prospective employer. We try to impress, or make an impression on, others by emphasizing something about ourselves that we think may appeal to them. When I dress smartly, have a ready smile, show confidence as I walk with my head up, or speak intelligently or articulately, I hope my demeanor will say positive things about me.

Or, we can receive an impression, either visual or emotional, from a landscape, an artwork, a novel, that is vague rather than specific. It will bring a different response from each individual thus impressed.

We speak of a fleeting impression of something in passing that is no longer there with us. And some impressions are indeed temporary. A drop of water falling into a still pond leaves its impression in widening circles that soon vanish.

Some impressions last a lifetime. A great many such past experiences have left traces in my malleable memory. I continue to remember the impression I have of the wind on my face during a wild ferry ride out to the Scottish island of Iona under heavy, threatening skies, or the suffocating heat of an Australian bushfire so intense that the west-facing windows of our house grew too hot to touch and made it hard to breathe. Or the manner of a precise, scholarly English professor in college; I can't recall his name, but the mental image of his classroom deportment sticks with me. He would consistently challenge any vague or imprecise definition. He couldn't abide sloppy thinking or expression and would require us students to refine and reword our responses.

Another word, *influence*, can be used as either a noun or a verb and derives from the concept of something "in-flowing." It suggests a less direct, more gradual and lasting kind of persuasion or manipulation toward change. In the world of art, this is often the result of movements or schools of thought that sway new generations of artists, leading to fresh techniques or styles and experimental connections.

Each of these words may be applied to the way we, as people of faith, connect with society and culture. When I think of the combined power of almost any vigorous group of artists and thinkers, and the difference they can make by their graphics, their writing, their thinking, their personal influence and conviction, I am electrified, energized.

Perhaps you are reading this because you wonder what you, one individual in a society of others, are called to do with your gift, and the sense of what life is opening up for you if you are available to it. If so, consider this.

An image, after all, is a likeness with a difference. It is close enough to what it stands for that we recognize the similarity, but also the difference. Both the similarity and the variation are important. They shift our thinking the way a moving van might shift our belongings from one location to another. (In fact, the Greek word for moving van is translated as "metaphor"!) You are an image of God, with a difference from all others. It is your responsibility to reflect that image in the most authentic way you can.

Have you noticed that whenever a little sunlight gleams during a dark day it marks and lifts our mood? When I sit in the sun, I sometimes feel as though the light is imprinting my skin, first with a feeling of brightness and warmth and, if I allow it a little time, darkening it, as the protective pigment melanin is activated in my epithelium.

And that's just the skin, the outside of us. We are imprinted in multiple ways—physically, spiritually, psychologically; by bruises, by surprises, by revelations, by happiness, by wounds and scars, by relationships with the people in our lives, by trauma and, in the end, as I am beginning to understand, by time and age.

I used to have a firm handshake, but now arthritis has weakened that gesture. My hands are bony and age-spotted.

Old Hand

The plum blue veins embroider their way
through a shrinkage of tissue, a lacing

of vines sucking at an unseen reservoir.
I touch my parchment skin, pushing it sideways
with the gentle forefinger of the other hand
and the pale tendons gleam like ivory
over the backdrop of murky muscle.

Across a keyboard the fingers flicker,
dedicated, busy with words that are concentrating
on imaginings larger than hinged metacarpals
or a minor mountain range of knuckles.
Made for work, curving to the keys, necessary adjuncts
to language, bridges from the brain.

My eyes are sharp and attentive. I still see clearly but my ophthalmologist has prescribed eye drops to ward off the possibility of glaucoma. I've begun to wear glasses when I'm driving at night so that I can see the street signs and avoid jaywalking pedestrians. I've been forced to use hearing aids if I'm to enter a lively conversation, which means the constant need to change the tiny size-ten batteries as they lose power. They are such cunning little devices, even more important than earrings. One of them to remedy deficiency, the other to suggest that ears were made for piercing!

Human experience marks us indelibly. And underlying all such imprints, our very DNA is the result of divine imprinting that makes us what and who we are in this created universe—generated, distinct, unique.

In my study some weeks ago I was surprised once again by how the sun speaks into me. The crystal pendant that's been hanging for years by a fishline in my study window was the lens for revelation; that morning as I was reading, the light struck through it, flooding the walls and carpet with rainbow light:

Prism

Through window glass the sun crosses my shoulder,
condensing into a small beetle of rainbow
that creeps along a line of type on the left page of
my novel, with its description of the protagonist's

facial expression. What seconds ago was
an adjective in a field of violet is now suffused
with yellow verging on neon green,
dyes so intense they stain my thumbnail,

turn mere knots of letters into signal flares.
Now the beetle is bridging the book's
gutter to tour the next page across a patch
of dialog and, curious about what comes next,
prepares to tumble its radiance off the far right
edge of the paper onto my wrist bone. Small envoy
of colored light, write your story on my skin.

I suspect we've each been printed on in multiple ways. For instance, how do memories from childhood affect your actions and reactions later in life? I vividly remember the family picnics by an Ontario waterfall, with my mother's "egg and bacon pie" (her version of a quiche) and watercress sandwiches, delicate triangles made *without the crusts*! As a result, all picnics since have an aura of fun and deliciousness for me, despite ants, flies and mosquitoes. Quiches are still a favorite to prepare and eat. Mother's recipe for "French steak" (a kind of ragout) was such a favorite with me and all my children that the printed recipe is being handed down the generations. I can almost taste it as I write!

Another impression from a long ago memory. In our early youth my brother and I were required to eat our crusts. And we both hated crusts, no matter how good the bread was or how lavishly slathered with butter. Our dining room table (and we ate all our meals sedately at that table, using our linen napkins and silverware) was rectangular, with a kind of shelf underneath where tabletop and supports met. I can still remember the sly way we would both palm our crusts after eating out the slices' soft interiors and slide them under the table edge and onto the shelf while maintaining interested eye contact and conversation with our parents. The truth was only revealed when we sold the house and moved the table, spilling its dusty load for all to see.

I remember how I conquered my preadolescent panic about sailing, when my dad outfitted a small, gaff-rigged sailboat by installing airtight canisters under the deck to prevent capsizing. Thereafter my brother and I could spend summer days sailing safely on Ontario's Muskoka Lakes. I look back at teenage canoe trips and still feel in memory the ache of shoulders straining in the hot sun and learning to cope with the emergency of capsizing and drenching our food supplies and sleeping bags. Such recollections feel indelible many decades later. And I still have my canoeing muscles.

I have been impressed by stories that retain their colors and shapes in our minds, our dreams. By words spoken, either in affirmation or dismissal or abuse. Sermons. Dramatic readings. Searching questions in a lecture hall. Speeches. Rants. Political protests. Quiet but memorable conversations around a dinner table with friends. Prayers together.

I am imprinted particularly by the words of Scripture in the King James Version as I heard them read aloud and expounded every Sunday in church in my youth, as I memorized passages for a Sunday school prize, so much so that I can almost always visualize the location of a specific verse in its place in my old Bible—left page, right-hand column, two-thirds of the way down. A word or phrase has burned its way into my memory, and my life. (I've concluded that the Hebrew word *Selah*, whose meaning has not been precisely determined, means this to me: "Stop and let this thought settle into your mind, and print it with your own personal meaning.")

I know where all the books of the Bible are, in sequence, because I'm imprinted with the song we learned as children to help us memorize the list: "Genesis, Exodus, Leviticus, Numbers . . ." to a catchy, singsongy hymn tune. Friends are especially impressed that I can rattle off the names of the minor prophets in one long unpunctuated mash-up! I was imprinted, like most of us as children, with the English alphabet, reciting the letters forward or backwards. And the French and Spanish alphabets. And the Greek, from my New Testament studies in college.

Memory is an amazing imprinting tool, another evidence of humanity's uniqueness. It's not only words that we are capable of remembering, but music (we count on this as we rehearse the tricky passages of anthems in our church choir; it's only when practice has firmly imprinted them in our minds that we can let the music take hold of us and sing freely and confidently). And smell and touch. The aroma of that early morning coffee. Of sweet hay being cut in a summer meadow. Tiger balm on an aching muscle. Lavender from my friend Lydia's garden. The feel of a cool shower on a hot, muggy day. Or, in winter, the warmth of hot chocolate by a log fire in the company of friends.

The more I reflect on "the marks of the Maker," the more I realize I am actively engaged in the imprinting process. Amazed, after all those primitive years of typewriters and carbons and correction fluid to correct typos, of mimeographing (accompanied by the unpleasant smell of the purple-inked sheets of paper as they were peeled off the printing drum), now replaced by photocopying and offset printing. My digital printer sits patiently in my study, waiting for me to press, happily and effortlessly, a rapid series of keys so that a blank sheet of paper a couple of feet away is primed to receive meaningful marks, black and colored signs and symbols, letters and words and vivid images that are there to be saved for the future and decoded for meaning.

I lift up my house phone or my smartphone and press buttons in a special sequence that connects me with a friend on the opposite coast of the continent.

Like Obadiah Parker in Flannery O'Connor's magical story "Parker's Back," I've been tattooed.[1] This happened several years ago in Vancouver on a visit with my friend Karen to the Sacred Heart of Jesus Tattoo and Piercing Parlor, where with the tattoo artist, a former Catholic altar boy, we unexpectedly engaged in a long conversation about sacred symbols as he worked with ink and needles on our bare skin. I had chosen a design already, and he had traced it out on the carbon transfer film used for the preliminary sketch to be inscribed on my upper arm. I had selected the likeness of a dogwood flower, *Cornus canadensis*, which is for me an emblem of Christ, with its four white petals stained at their tips with crimson. A Christ blossom. A spring flower full of grace for me. A constant bodily reminder to be true to that image. A much earlier poem of mine had probably informed my choice of this design:

Rising, the Underground Tree

One spring in Tennessee, I walked a tunnel
under dogwood trees, noting the petals
(in fours, like crosses) and at each tender apex

four russet stains dark as Christ-wounds.
I knew that with the year the dogwood flower heads
would ripen into berry clusters bright as drops of gore.

Last week, a double-click on Botany
startles me with the kinship of those trees
with bunch berries, whose densely crowded mat

carpets the deep woods around my cabin.
Only their flowers — those white quartets of petals
Suggest the blood relationship. Since then I see

the miniature leaves and buds as tips of trees
burgeoning underground, knotted roots like limbs
Pushing up to light through rock and humus.

The pure cross flowers at my feet redeem
their long, dark burial underground,
show how even a weight of stony soil
cannot keep Easter at bay.

Last spring I visited another tattoo artist closer to home in Bellingham and had another dogwood flower bud, stalk and leaves added to the first tattoo, which had faded a bit. He pinked in the tips of the petals and greened in the leaves. In the summer, when sleeves are shorter, my tattoo brings me comments of both admiration and horror.

In Flannery O'Connor's narrative "Parker's Back," what happened on the back of Parker, her protagonist, was a kind of resurrection, a new Easter, as the image of Christ was permanently emblazoned on his skin by a tattoo artist. Where before, Obadiah Parker, in an unsuccessful attempt to soothe his unsatisfied soul, had filled all the empty spaces on the skin on the front of his body with a blurred jumble of insignificant signs and symbols, now, even in the face of his wife Sarah Ruth's cry of "Idolatry!" he'd added a new image. After receiving it on his back he knew he'd experienced a kind of beatific vision.

In keeping with his prophet's name, Obadiah, "all at once he felt the light pouring through him, turning his spider web soul into a perfect arabesque of colors, a garden of trees and birds and beasts." Reading this, perhaps one of O'Connor's most lyrical descriptions of possibility, I saw a kind of Eden, a new beginning, the possibility of a fresh start for this failure of a man.

In O'Connor's story, the beckoning of the transcendent had been going on for some time, with Parker resisting all the way.

An incident that took place in the field of his employer, a farmer, had quickened the pace of his passage toward grace. He had wrecked the machine with which he'd been baling hay, circling closer and closer to the meadow's ancient, central tree until he had crashed into it. During this circuit he was profoundly aware of the sun, the size of a golf ball, as it began to switch regularly from in front to behind him until he ran into the tree, upended the baler and saw it, along with the tree itself, burst into flames. He'd been thrown free of the machine, but one shoe fell off and the other caught fire, leaving him barefooted (like Moses before the burning bush). He'd run away, sure that he'd lose his job because of his stupidity. "He only knew that there had been a great change in his life, a leap forward into a worse unknown, and that there was nothing he could do about it." The relentless tug of the divine was intensified. Events had to turn worse for him before they could change for the better.

His past response, in any time of dissatisfaction, had always been to get a new tattoo. Hoping to impress his wife, a woman possessed by a kind of strangling religiosity, he searched the tattoo artist's pattern book for a design, and one in particular arrested him. "On one of the pages a pair of eyes glanced at him swiftly. Parker sped on, then stopped. . . . There was absolute silence. It said as plainly as if silence were a language itself, GO BACK."

The tug of the grace of God was proving irresistible. The image of the Byzantine Christ that he'd then had tattooed on his back was like an icon, "whose eyes penetrated him like the sun"—an image of the new covenant and all it promised. Sarah Ruth, his wife, was wedded to the Old Covenant with its demanding and condemning law; she was always "sniffing out sin" without searching for or finding its opposite.

Once again, unlike Moses, who descended from Sinai after seeing "the back parts of Yahweh" with his face veiled so that the people couldn't see that the glory was fading, Parker finally removes his shirt to show his back to his wife, but she retorts that God is a spirit and this representation of Christ's face is idolatry. She begins to beat him until he is knocked senseless and on his skin large welts form on the face of the tattooed Christ. She, dense and ugly and righteous, has refused to recognize divine grace. Parker ends up violently ousted from her house, "leaning against the tree, crying like a baby." It's the tree where, significantly, he finds a place of sorrow and penitence.

Paul tells us in Romans to "clothe yourselves with the Lord Jesus Christ" (Romans 13:14 NIV) and in Colossians to be clothed with "compassion, kindness, humility" (Colossians 3:12 NIV). Earlier in Colossians we may get the remarkable sense of being impregnated, "Christ *in you*, the hope of glory" (Colossians 1:27 NIV). The imprint of Christ on us has to be deeper, more profound, than any tattoo. We may wear a cross, we may hang icons in our offices, we may be members of a religious order, but we had better live into the truth of those symbols if they are to have meaning to us or anyone else.

I'm reminded of the story Annie Dillard tells in *Holy the Firm*. During the seven years that she taught at Western Washington University in Bellingham, she lived on Lummi Island, one of the San Juan Islands just a brief ferry ride from our mainland. She regularly attended the island's little white Congregational church. I have visited the island often, and the church building is still there. Dillard describes the Sunday when she was assigned the job of bringing the Communion wine, as she walked to church with the bottle "in a sack *on her back.*" Like Parker, whose being was irradiated with the image of Christ, Annie describes how the wine in the bottle on her back began to imprint her soul and body. In this fragment from a poem titled "Two Stanzas: The Eucharist," I describe how I interpreted this incident:

Annie Dillard speaks of Christ
Corked in a bottle: carrying the wine
To communion in a pack on her back
She feels him lambent, lighting
Her hidden valleys through the spaces
Between her ribs. Nor can we
Contain him in a cup. He is always
Poured out for our congregation.

We may ask ourselves, how are we Christ-imprinted? What is God calling us to do and be as we stand awed and fearful before some significantly burning bush? What needs to happen for us to receive some kind of stigmata—signals that mark us as Christ's own, not, perhaps, the bloody wounds in the palms of the hands but the pure, open, joyful and contrite heart that God has promised to claim for himself, to not despise and to count as more valuable to him than any human accomplishment and success?

seven

Seals of Authenticity

*O*n a recent river trip down the Rhine, from Amsterdam to Basel, we anchored on a German shore for a bus trip to Heidelberg, a city with all the marks of its history clearly evident. High over the city is the castle, with its ancient moat and high walls. As we entered through the castle's arched portal, I noticed that each of the huge blocks of stone used in its construction had a symbol chipped into its surface. I leaned closer, photographing it so as not to forget it. On inquiry I learned that the masons, hoping for their skill to be remembered, had each left an individual mark on every stone that they had hewn out of the rockface of the mountain. Centuries later, though the stonemasons are long gone, the marks are clear.

We are said to be "living stones" in the building of faith. We have each been marked specifically, each of us unique within the human race. With all the ways that creation, including our own human component of that creation, is imprinted by God, a thumbprint remains for me the most available, visible and useful identifying mark. I value its capability. Its way of depicting identity and uniqueness reminds me of a seal—that which fastens shut or firmly marks. When I pay my bills and write a check and slip it in an envelope, I lick the glued edge, press it down and keep pressing until I'm sure that a strong seal has been made and I drop it in the mailbox.

Okay. Let's look back inside that envelope at the check with my signature on it, and recognize that my written name authenticates the fact that I am paying my bills and being responsible for my expenses. Granted that my signature, like that of many others, may look like an incoherent scribble, that name is my seal and my promise. And even the flourish of ink that stands for my name is pretty much the same whenever I sign a document.

Because every individual's signature is different, handwriting experts believe that they can even determine personality traits by analyzing the slant and configurations of a sample of someone's writing. This system, graphology, often thought of as a pseudoscience, has nevertheless been used to detect forgeries, especially on legal documents, and is seen as an indicator of certain tendencies on the part of the writer. For instance, some analysts see Georgia O'Keeffe's squiggles and erratic style as indicative of an iconoclastic personality.

Penmanship used to be taught in schools. In the 1850s and on, the style promoted by Platt Rogers Spencer made for grace and legibility. One popular style was known as copper-plate, the flowing and elegant cursive style that was encouraged in the Victorian age of the nineteenth century. A delicate, even spidery hand, carefully spaced and inscribed, indicated an educated, refined writer. To conserve paper, a costly commodity at the time, some of these letter writers wrote both horizontally across the page, then vertically, up and down, and because of their faultless penmanship their messages were still perfectly legible.

Before pens had their own barrels of ink, and long before felt-tip or roller-ball pens came into use, nibs were cut in the quills of feathers, and the resulting writing had the light and dark elements that were formed by light or heavy thumb and finger pressure. I have some of these letters from missionary great aunts and uncles, the paper and ink both faded but the writing perfectly legible. Over the years calligraphers developed multiple styles of writing, from which some of our current typefaces derive.

The doctor's notes on prescription pads are predictably indecipherable, usually scribbled in a hurry as the physician leaves the patient's examination room. We pray that the pharmacist gets the message right. My son John, a doctor himself, is an exception, with neat, precise writing that goes along with his skilled medical illustrations. I've noticed that standard styles of handwriting vary between countries, such as Australia and England. My mother, from New Zealand, had a beautiful, rounded, elegant hand. She wrote to me every day while I was away in college, and I was expected to write back. My hurried notes written between classes or back in my dorm room were, by contrast, uneven and inelegant. My father's writing was spiky, minuscule and almost indecipherable, in dark blue ink. Likely because of this my mother, whose devotion perhaps enabled her to be the only one who could read Dad's letters, emphasized *good* handwriting. (In memory of him, I have saved scraps of letters written to me when I was in college. I *think* I know what he said; he was a very loving father!) Though it is still recognizably mine, my own handwriting has not improved with age, probably because of my habit of scrawling entries in my journal on the run or scribbling in bed in the dark (when an idea has arrived and I feel for the journal and pen on my night table in hopes of recording a phrase or idea so that its potency will persist until morning light). I keep a miniature notebook in my purse, and if I have an idea while waiting in the checkout line at the supermarket I can jot it down, to be deciphered later. Left-handed writers face a somewhat different challenge in a right-handed society. Since three of my children are southpaws, I've seen this struggle firsthand.

With the invention of typewriters and now with all the lovely varieties of digital fonts used in word processing, handwriting has become almost a thing of the past. I occasionally send a postcard. I still write my checks. Almost everyone has a printer available. We can set a certain font as our default. My favorites are Book Antiqua and Palatino.

We may seal a promise with a kiss and a hug. Or a business agreement with a firm handshake. We pay attorneys enormous hourly fees when we sign legal papers like wills or contracts in their offices, or have them duly witnessed in the presence of a certified public accountant, with an embossed seal to attest to their authenticity. I have a friend who still seals his envelopes with red sealing wax impressed with his initial.

Thinking along these lines of promises and authenticity, I've been struck by the great Old Testament example given in the message of the prophet Haggai, in which God pronounces that he will make Zerubbabel his "signet ring." Zerubbabel, though not a king, was the governor or civil leader of the fragmented nation of Israel during the time when the city of Jerusalem was being rebuilt following the peoples' return from the Babylonian captivity.

This was the proclamation: "The word of the LORD came a second time to Haggai on the twenty-fourth day of the month: Speak to Zerubbabel, governor of Judah, saying, I am about to shake the heavens and the earth, and to overthrow the throne of kingdoms; I am about to destroy the strength of the kingdoms of the nations" (Haggai 2:20-22). (Talk about the impact of God's thumbprint! A Hasidic saying goes like this: "God is not an uncle. God is an earthquake." In a similar vein, Canadian writer Murray Pura once warned an audience that "Jesus is not a glass of milk.") The power that shaped the universe is evident in the shaking, the disruption.

"On that day . . . I will take you, O Zerubbabel, . . . as my personal servant and I will set you *as a signet ring*, the sign of my sovereign presence and authority. . . . I've . . . chosen you for this work" (Haggai 2:23 *The Message*).

Zerubbabel's name means "son of Babylon" because the pagan city of Babylon was his birthplace. Yet as part of Israel's faithful remnant—the ones who maintained their devotion to Yahweh during their time in exile—he was the one who returned to the ruined, decimated Jerusalem and supervised the laying of the foundations of the second temple.

I am awed by the significance of the very direct and definite role assigned to Zerubbabel. It seems to prefigure the responsibility that Christian writers, artists, thinkers and theologians may claim in society, of guiding an errant or complacent population in the rebuilding of an authentic relationship with God. The way we worship, work, communicate, create and exert influence defines us as change-makers in society. We form the seal. Like Zerubbabel, we may *become* the seal.

Such an authenticating symbol, impressed in wax or a clay tablet, or in Zerubbabel's day in vegetable ink on parchment, was the proof of authenticity. Today's copyright symbol—©—

applied next to the texts of our books and poems, our films and essays, testifies that the words and the way the work is presented are original, that they are ours alone.

In the larger sphere it's as if that ancient seal of authority has been granted to us to rebuild what, like Solomon's glorious temple, has been eroded or dismantled in Christendom and in the secularization of culture and a politicized and technocratic world.

Since the Enlightenment, the cynicism and skepticism that has infected the church is evident in the schisms and conflicts wherever we look. This is true among many denominations. I'm an Episcopalian, and segments of the worldwide Anglican Communion have been in flux, determinedly trying to find their identity in the midst of conflicting understandings of what the church is called to be and do in our own time. But the obligatory piety of the Victorian age, the "death of God" movement, the deconstructionism of Derrida and Foucault and the related postmodernism, the commercialization of the sacred, the pluralism of belief or unbelief, the degrading of moral values, the democratization of excellence, and the erosion of what used to be called "absolute" have all effected shifts in human understandings of meaning. The result: the significance of the sacred sometimes seems like a ravaged parchment or a garbled, coded memorandum without a key. Add to that the exponential speed at which communication is happening, demanding our constant attention to the urgencies of the Internet, which seldom rewards care and concentration in our thinking. The result of this erosion may cast a blanket of confusion about what we are called to do and be as Christian believers.

When we look closely at what Yahweh was saying through his prophet Haggai, we see something very much like this: "I am extending my authority through you, Zerubbabel, so that you may make *my mark* on your people."

But how was this "marking" to begin and continue? Not only was Zerubbabel one of the ancestors of Jesus the Messiah, extending God's authority as manifested through him to proclaim a new covenant, to change the world—the whole human race as well as the Jewish nation—but that seal of divine authority has been passed on to us by Christ himself to make a mark on our own culture, many centuries later. "Go out and train everyone you meet, far and near, in this way of life" (Matthew 28:19 *The Message*).

How are we ourselves imprinted by God, beyond being "made in his image" with intellect, emotions and will? I believe human beings, with our self-consciousness, our capability for abstract thought, our ability to observe and pay attention to the significant details of the real world, our hunger for both wisdom and knowledge, our use of language and story, our sense of the transcendent, our moral sense of right and wrong, have a unique place in creation. (Years ago the *New Yorker* ran an article on young children's intuitive grasp of the supernatural, a sensitivity that seems to have been lost in many adults.)

This opens up a deep, personal, practical contact between deity and the human being. God doesn't simply wave his hand in our direction and expect a robotic response. His touch, his imprint, is firmly and continually felt if we pay attention. If we listen with ever-opening ears. If we train ourselves to recognize an impulse that bridges the gap between deity and humanity that gives us a unitive voice. Between my God and me, in our oneness. It is our souls and spirits that feel the impact, which *were created to feel the impact*, and respond to it. Here's a fragment from a recent poem of mine:

Maestro

I love god not as
the conductor of a distant
orchestra that makes of
the universe a band
shell and space an acoustic
device but god who
takes me by the wrist
firmly and points ahead.

We have been told that as believers we are Christ's body—a startling thought. The immediacy of it is electrifying. Mary bore the body of Christ. We *are* the body. In truth, we human beings incarnate Jesus as his Spirit enters and directs us.

As biblical Christians we have heard this analogy—of a motley bunch of believing people making up the earthly body of Christ—so often and for so long that the fleshy image has become over-familiar, has lost its potency. Yet when we step back from our comfortable theology, the physicality of this metaphor is disturbing. It is also enlightening. In that body I may be a fingernail, but you may be an eye or an ear or a mouth. An eyelash. A penis. A neuron in a cerebral cortex, a tooth, an ovary, an artery, an ankle bone, a toenail. A wrinkle in aging skin.

It makes us ask, "Is it possible for us to be the hands and fingers and thumbs that mold our friends and neighbors, our colleagues, our readers and writers, and beyond them, the culture at large, in a way that reflects the truth about our Maker?"

The Partaking (addressed to God)

Bread of the Presence
was, in Moses' day
served on engraved gold plates
to You and Your select few.
And in exclusive glory
one alone and lonely man
sprinkled, with fear,
the ceremonial drops that pleaded

failure for another year
to You, known then
as only high and holy —
heavens apart from common
women, common men.
Often we taste the
granular body of wheat
(Think of the Grain that was buried
and died!)
and swallow together
the grape's warm, burning blood
(Remembering First Fruit!)
knowing ourselves a part of you
as you took part of us, flowed
in our kind of veins
quickened cells like ours
into a human subdividing:
now you are multiplied —
we are your fingers and your feet,
your tender heart — we
are your broken side.
Take now, and crumble small,
and cast our human bread on
the world's waters, your contemporary
Showbread. Feed us
to more than five thousand women and men

and in our dark, daily flood of living
pour yourself out again.

So. The holy Presence becomes part of our quotidian living. We may shape the culture by service, by compassion, by engagement in political or humanitarian movements, by peacemaking, by teaching, by ideas, by words, by stories, by the way our thumbprints touch and change who and what we are connected with. By being who we are called by God to be. This is likely to happen one person at a time. But one and one and one can multiply in the same way that the cells in an amoeba divide and ultimately form a whole body.

Imagery and story are God's chosen teaching tools, God's soft-sell sales pitch. His purpose and method is to inform human beings through images and narratives and histories and dreams, working to awaken our imaginations—that part of all of us that responds through the senses of perception and their ability to form pictures in our heads. Propositions may convince our intellectual faculties, but pictures awaken our imaginations. They stick in our memories like tattoos on skin.

We sometimes fail to recognize that one-third of the Bible is in the form of poetry. Read Genesis 1 aloud and listen to its pure poetry, its repeating cadences. (Who was the poet here? Was it the collaborative work of the Holy Spirit with a human scribe? Was it Moses, traditionally thought to be the author of the Pentateuch? Was it any one of the many translators working from the Hebrew text?) The Psalms, Ecclesiastes and many of the prophetic writings come to us in the form of Hebraic poetry, with its parallelism, its repetitive structure. We trust that Holy Writ was writ under the guiding influence of the Spirit, employing a brilliant array of metaphors, similes and images to bring home to us the substance of the stories, proclamations and teachings.

Many of these images are sensuous. "As the deer *longs* for flowing streams, so my soul longs for you, O God" (Psalm 42:1). In Hosea 14:5-6 Yahweh uses natural imagery to reassure his people: "I will be *like the dew* to Israel; he shall blossom like the lily . . . his fragrance like a cedar of Lebanon" (NIV). And again, when he asks, "What have [you] to do with idols? . . . *I* am like an evergreen cypress" (Hosea 14:8). That is, *my leaves will not fall, nor my provisions fail. I am green and fruitful in every season.* To receive the truth of this divine declaration we must sense our way into the reality of an evergreen tree. In many of the places I've lived, evergreens, sometimes the sequoias and redwoods of California, or the Douglas firs and hemlocks and cedars and spruces of the Northwest, have colored in for me the lines of the scriptural figure of speech. Even the piney smell alerts me to God's presence.

David, the songwriter, Israel's poet and psalm singer, proclaimed in Psalm 52:8 that he was like "a green olive tree in the house of God"—an olive tree full of oil and sap and fruit, its leafy arms raised in praise to the Lord. I've seen the groves of olive trees in Greece and Israel and California. Squat and rugged with the bulk of long life and still capable of bearing fruit.

Much imagery has become a cliché. What was once a colorful and resonant image has become dusty and feeble through overuse. "Dead as a doornail." "Happy as a clam." "Over the hill." The French word *cliché* means "key," an image that unlocks a figure of speech to bring new meaning. We make comparisons and say something is "as flat as a pancake." "As old as the hills." "As soft as silk." "More fun than a barrel of monkeys." We compare and contrast to get at the heart of a thing's meaning. But the zing of it, the fresh understanding that may come through comparison often loses its freshness. We dampen it through overfamiliarity. It is up to us to invent new metaphors and analogies to bring truer meanings into our conversations.

A biblical example of imagery is in the Song of Songs, Solomon's erotic meditation on his lover whom he describes as so irresistibly beautiful that she is to him "terrible as an army with banners." Her beauty has overwhelmed him. This is wonderfully hyperbolic, but even if we do not take it literally it shapes our understanding of divine love. In unpacking this allegorical outpouring, the object of the writer's fervor has been likened to the city of Jerusalem, as well as to Christ's bride, the church. Thoughtfully read and pondered, without casually coasting over them in our thinking, such images can come to life again and become forceful, words from God that penetrate our hearts.

Here's another image, one of many hundreds of promises in Isaiah: "Though your sins are like scarlet, they shall be as white as snow; though they are red as crimson, they shall be like wool" (Isaiah 1:18 NIV). Abstract that idea, turn it into a proposition that proclaims, "God can change and cleanse you," a reality which, though true enough, has somehow lost its punch, the energy of the image. It needs the color and contrast and texture of blood versus snow and wool to print our imaginations with its intense truth. God, who created our minds and imaginations, knows also how to stir them into response.

The prophet Ezekiel not only proclaimed his unearthly visions, he lived his metaphors, sometimes reluctantly, but with a kind of vivid veracity that left no doubt about the force of the message. He was told, in the precise, no-nonsense words of Scripture,

> You, O mortal, take a brick and set it before you. By it portray a city, Jerusalem. . . . Set your face toward it, and let it be in a state of siege. . . . This is a sign for the house of Israel.
>
> Then lie on your left side, and place the punishment of the house of Israel upon it. . . . I assign to you . . . three hundred ninety days, equal to the number of the

years of their punishment; and so you shall bear [their] punishment. . . . When you have completed these, you shall lie down a second time, but on your right side, and bear the punishment of the house of Judah; forty days I assign you, one day for each year. . . . See, I am putting cords on you so that you cannot turn from one side to the other until you have completed the days of your siege. (Ezekiel 4:1-8)

During these days of forceful bodily restriction Ezekiel was told to bake bread for his daily sustenance on the fire of his own dung. (When he protested, understandably, that in traditional Jewish practice this would make him unclean, Yahweh relented and allowed him to use cow dung instead!) For the onlookers it was an uncompromising message. Difficult to proclaim and equally difficult to attend to. Ezekiel also metaphorically described the corruption of Israel as repulsive as "a basket of rotten figs."

Our art, in writing or graphic visual imagery, may well need to be offensive in the sense of shocking. Harsh. Stark. Jesus' indictment of empty, Pharisaical religiosity was like a blow to the pit of the stomach of the religious leaders of the day. It was voiced in comparisons that likened those legalistic leaders to whitewashed tombs full of decaying bodies. Jesus was saying, "I smell your rottenness." His hyperbolic language about cutting off one's hand or gouging out one's eye was meant to shock, to sting, to jolt his hearers, and us, with the impact of an idea that might change our lives. Warnings. Challenges. Impossibilities.

The Foolishness of God

Perform impossibilities
or perish. Thrust out now
the unseasonal ripe figs
among your leaves. Expect
the mountain to be moved.
Hate parents, friends, and all
materiality. Love every enemy.
Forgive more times than seventy-
seven. Camel-like, squeeze by
into the kingdom through
the needle's eye. All fear quell.
Hack off your hand, or else,
unbloodied, go to hell.

Thus the divine unreason.
Despairing, you may cry,
with earthy logic — How?
And I, your God, reply:
Leap from your weedy shallows.
Dive into the moving water.
Eye-less, learn to see

truly. Find in my folly your
true sanity. Then, Spirit-driven,
run on my narrow way, sure
as a child. Probe, hold
my unhealed hand, and
bloody, enter heaven.

There is an established link between the immanent earthly, the palpably coarse, the physically, biologically authentic, and the realities of the eternal transcendent, all of which lie beyond our grasp, our control, our view, our comprehension but whose reality we have been led to believe is bound up with that of the physical world. This is a mystery—something hidden and yet to be revealed. Sometimes it is only metaphorically that we can glimpse the "unseen real," that which may be obscure to our physical eyes but which our Creator gave us imaginations to penetrate.

For me, a definition of *epiphany* is "the unveiling of a mystery," like a beam of sun shining through mist. Our eyes, both physical and spiritual, were designed to be open to light. To accept and decode it. To let it radiate into us and through us.

One fall I was invited by Leonard Sweet to attend what was called a Mountain Advance—the opposite of a retreat—in West Virginia. I was to be there specifically as a poet, a resource for a group of pastors and theologians, to search for fresh metaphors to use in the proclamation of the gospel. Sweet, of Drew University, with his Free Methodist background, rather than using the term *denominations*, talks about religious *tribes*: "My tribe emphasizes this. . . . His tribe is going in *that* direction." He decries the ubiquitous model of "leadership" that has evolved in the last several decades, but sees the need for *iconic figures* such as Gandhi, Pope Francis, Bishop Tutu, Martin Luther King Jr., Bono, Nelson Mandela, Bill and Melinda Gates, Mother Teresa, all of whom have had the capability of transforming the culture by example and by force of personality.

We discussed how the Holy Spirit is often seen as Paraclete, Comforter, words that project a valid biblical image of support, help and compassion. But according to Sweet, the word *advocate* may also mean "the warrior who watches my back"—a protector in a fierce conflict.

Such fresh language can help us see a biblical image with new eyes. But we must be prepared to open our eyes, to move from what has become a well-worn bit of dogma in our minds to a vivid picture vigorous enough to freshen a relationship with God.

Again and again I have to ask myself about my ability to receive the image and imprint of the Creator, "Am I sand or sawdust? Stone, or malleable, fireable wax or clay? Am I adventurous enough to accept a new version of a familiar directive in Scripture? Have I asserted my own selfhood to such a degree that I'm impenetrable, unwilling to acknowledge God's redemptive ownership of me and any gift I have? Does the thumbprint of my life and writing show any evidence of its origin? Its etymology?"

A modern rendering of Psalm 31:12 goes like this: "I feel as useless as a broken pot."[1] From time to time, as political pressures and social shifts occur, we may feel tempted to see our own small imprint as too trivial or insignificant to make a difference, leaving no discernible trace. We may fall back into a sense of failure and passivity. We may dismiss personal initiatives as ineffective.

Once, while driving through the Midwest, I passed a large roadside billboard that advised, "If you can't be kind, be vague." The concept of speaking with truth and precision, even charitably . . . forget it. Overcome your impulse to speak up about something that needs correction. I wanted to respond, "In that case, why bother to express yourself at all?"

But think of the way visionaries and artists of faith have touched the world, some well known, some obscure. Botticelli, Dürer, da Vinci, Titian, Michelangelo, Rembrandt and his *Prodigal Son*. The illuminated pages of the Books of Kells and the Lindisfarne Gospels, among many other ancient manuscripts, preserved God-words for future generations with such magnificence. And Bach, in his little church in Leipzig, writing choral music to accompany the story of Jesus' death as told in Matthew's Gospel. The metaphysical poets Donne,

Crashaw, Herbert, Hopkins. Mel Gibson dramatizing the gospel account in film. *The Jesus Film*. The cathedrals and monasteries of the world. Assisi and San Damiano and San Marco. The monks and nuns who live their closeted lives to work and pray for the life of the world. Add your own examples to the brilliant list.

Here's how a memorable imprint was made on me when recently I had opportunity to go to Romania with poet Jeanne Murray Walker. Both Jeanne and I are members of the Chrysostom Society, a group of Christian writers who, for the past nearly thirty years, have been committed to making an imprint on culture by writing challenging books, essays, plays and poetry. The two of us were invited by a group of about twenty-five Romanian poets of faith, led by writer Ionatan Pirosca, to come and lead a writing workshop with them in the university city of Cluj. They felt isolated from Western culture and literature, and together, we and they hoped to bridge a bit of that gap.

Since the downfall of Ceauşescu in 1989, the national churches in Romania have largely become so politicized and corrupt that it is hard for heartfelt Christian belief to flourish in them. But small independent communities of faith are springing up, and among them the work of these poets is beginning to make a difference as part of this new wave of Christian conviction, in their own lives and communities and in the anthologies of poetry that they are publishing.

For four days we met with them to lecture, exchange poems, discuss the poetic process, critique individual work and do what we could to encourage them. Both Jeanne and I were commissioned by our individual Episcopal congregations as a form of international outreach.

It has been said that "every Romanian is a poet." These are passionate, gifted, generous, fearless, opinionated writers. As it turned out, Jeanne and I both felt that we gained much more from them than vice versa. They were poor in this world's goods but had put their resources together to put us up in a "two-star hotel" while they found lodging in the homes of local friends. Their courage, their enthusiasm and the quality of their work have to be seen to be believed. Since then we have been able to help translate and publish a number of their poems in American journals.

Every day for a week we met in the open air on a grassy plot of land behind church property. The biggest challenge: a two-way link had to be made between our language and theirs, our worldview and theirs, our life history and theirs. Of incalculable value was the help of a gifted Romanian colleague, Andreea Luncan, who has degrees in English literature and speaks flawless idiomatic English. Several other poet translators spent their days standing at our shoulders and quietly translating the conversations and discussions that were going on so that we could fully participate in the proceedings.

We were there also to attend the launch of a new volume

of their poetry, *Cuvinte la Schimb*, or *Words Exchange*, in the large university bookstore in the city. The Romanian minister of culture was invited to give a speech as part of the celebration, and he remarked how encouraging it was to celebrate "a poetry of hope rather than despair."

On a corner of a central intersection in Cluj stand six bronze pillars, erected as memorials to the six Romanian citizens who died during the coup against Ceaușescu. Varying between eight and ten feet tall, these metal columns are shaped and twisted and bear markings that represent abrasions and deep bullet holes. We reached up and were able, like Thomas, to put our fingers in the wounds. In feeling out the contours of that scarred metal, I felt as if I *were* Thomas, and that my own faith, often tested and wavering, was being restored.

These sculptures are the work of Liviu Mocan, an internationally known artist and sculptor whose Christian convictions have never been hidden. On a metal plate embedded in the pavement next to the bronzes at that Cluj city intersection are the words of Christ: "Greater love has no one than this, that one lay down his life for his friends." In the bustling, utterly secular city of Cluj, this stamp, this public seal of faith, impressed us indelibly.

At another crossroads, the intersection of faith and writing, you and I may be simply called to make our mark—some kind of X on the signature line—or to send a first-class letter with a first-class postage stamp. We trust that our poems, essays, stories and sermons will leave an imprint on those who read our words or hear our convictions. We may be asked to make prints from large woodcuts or illuminated manuscripts that end up hung in national galleries, sculptures that may be seen by thousands. Or a small poem that ends up in a magazine that speaks something fresh and life changing to a reader. Culture has a thousand surfaces that invite the stamp of meaning.

Never has it been so important as now for our own work, our calling, to be authentic as our lives unfold, teaching us, marking us as we go, informing us and enriching us so that we ourselves, in our relationships and connections, with our words and our personal influence, may become seals, living texts, of God's thumbprint on our clay, indelible imprints visible to the world.

If God could shape an Adam out of mud or an Eve out of a thin bone, what might he do with us?

eight

Remarking, Remaking

*A*t a recent, pivotal intersection in my life I flew to Santa Fe, New Mexico, for a retreat at the Glen Workshop, the magnetic annual gathering that draws together artists and writers and music makers to mingle and practice their "spiritual disciplines"—whatever creative gift they exercise and hope to enliven.

My flight from Bellingham is a series of mishaps. Rising at 3:00 a.m., dopey with sleep and tense with the need to hurry, I feel miserably nauseated and spend the flight gratefully using the airsick bag in the seat pocket. There are missed connections on the flights south and in Phoenix a mix-up with the checked luggage. I continue to feel queasy as I chew on the complimentary banana chips and pretzels, hoping for a return of vigor.

Finally I arrive in Albuquerque, still feeling rocky. The temperature is in the high 90s. At a *really* cheapie car rental company, as I later discover, I've reserved a car for the hour-long drive north to Santa Fe. Fifteen minutes along the highway I develop *two* flat tires and have to wait hours in the searing heat for a tow truck. The rental agent, a gruff man, comes with the tow truck and shouts accusingly, claiming that as well as the flat tires there is front-end damage to the car that "must also have been my fault." I know this is untrue. After much unpleasant discussion back at the rental agency I get another car, and in my unsettled state find myself paying for tire replacement and body damage, not sure what insurance will cover even though none of it was my fault.

I begin to wonder. It all feels as if I am being deliberately impeded by "something" that is putting roadblocks in my way and discouraging me from getting to my destination. I keep thinking, *This must be important. I've got to push through it, and keep going.*

Persistence paid off, and late that evening, with the evening sun gleaming crimson over the mountains in the west, I finally arrive at St. John's College, in the high desert of Santa Fe, where the Glen West workshop is held every summer. After registration, I finally settle into my dorm room on campus.

At 2:00 a.m. that night on the way to the bathroom across the hall, I hear my door slam shut behind me, with the key inside. I am in my summer nightclothes and shivering. I decide to try to sleep lying on a bristly couch in the common room, covering myself and trying to keep warm with two large, bristly sofa pillows. After an hour of self-flagellation

at my carelessness about the key, I hesitantly knock on the
dorm door next to mine and ask its kindly, sleepy occupant
to call campus security. Soon I am back in my bed, relieved
but still wondering. This discouraging episode feels like an-
other obstacle.

Fr. Richard Rohr, a Franciscan friar and founder of the Center
for Action and Contemplation in Albuquerque, is our chaplain
for the week—an ample, alert, informal presence in his mud-
brown cassock. Close up Richard has blue, mirthful eyes. I've
heard of him for years, have contributed to books of Advent
and Lenten meditations along with him. I know that he is
articulate and that he sounds, from his writing, approachable.
In keeping with the Glen West theme for the year—"making
it new"—his evening meditations for the assembled artists
focus on the promise of "making all things new" and being
open to "the now." His words are simple, grace filled and
deeply thought provoking.

Richard exudes welcome, openness and optimism. What he
emphasizes feels possible, deeply desirable. Seeking wisdom, as
always, and somehow intrigued that his benedictions are offered
"in all the holy names of God," I feel impelled to ask him if we
can meet for an hour of conversation over lunch. Tomorrow.

I'm hoping that perhaps he can help me understand how to
integrate the discoveries of cosmologists about the immensity

of the universe since the initial "big bang" with the Christian story of Jesus' incarnation on our tiny fleck of a planet. Scientists are continually working to penetrate the mysteries of space and unlock the workings of time and matter as they affect the ongoing formation of the universe. Such searchings about unknown dimensions fascinate, almost mesmerize, me. I am no scientist, but I love to see how human intelligence builds on what is known to open up what is as yet unknown, pushing back the frontiers of knowledge. I long for assurance that all truth and the answers to human existence are to be found in the Creator of the universe. What I wanted was a kind of "theory of everything" that includes Christian faith.

Next day I spend the morning writing in my little dorm room, austere as a monastic cell, which is a great place to be without distraction. Around noon I walk to the college dining hall in the intense high desert heat, hungry for sustenance both physical and spiritual. Richard meets me in the cafeteria food line, and after picking up our salads we zero in on a table by a large window. It overlooks distant Santa Fe through the leaves of a poplar tree.

We are alone. For over an hour I sit face to face with this approachable wise man and talk. It is like opening a faucet. I pour out the story of my lifelong pursuit of God, a God I long to love freely and from whom I wish to sense a return of love. Mine is the old story of doubt and desire, of occasional flashes of light and renewal, of depression about my failure consistently to achieve the joy of the Lord and to trust that Lord unreservedly.

Sometimes, from the narrow boundaries of the rather primitive and very conservative theology of my youth, I'd wondered how I could break free. Could I leave it all behind and start again from scratch, move into being (gasp) "liberal," or even acknowledge a kind of agnosticism? Who would be my friends then? How would my family respond? Would I be sending my children the wrong message? But I lacked the gumption. Too much of my life had been built on this platform of doing the right thing, being the right kind of Christian and getting approved for it.

Richard hears me out. We are eye to eye and, I feel, heart to heart. A perceptive listener, he seems to understand immediately where my struggle lies. I explain how challenging it is for me to mentally integrate the advances being made by scientists—as they explore the mysteries of space and time, quantum physics, the ongoing investigation of the universe, reaching out trillions of light years in discovery and theory—with the tense theological constriction I've felt since childhood in the evangelical community of my upbringing, with its rules and ironclad principles that seemed to clog my heart rather than lift it.

To be required what to believe (and to never question it) had often felt crushing. These two worlds—science and the "fundamentalist" strictures about truth—have felt not only contradictory and impossible but unrelated. And now I want to be open to whatever reality God has for me. Though in my habit of life I'd been a faithful Christian for all my eighty-five years, my longing to feel a personal, divine love had never been truly satisfied. I've even written books voicing this disease of spiritual uncertainty. Am I just a complainer? A stubborn skeptic? What help can I find to combine points of view that had seemed incongruous. And is such integration even possible?

A series of spiritual directors, those companions of the soul, have nudged me to accept that the waverings of doubt and the flashes of light are simply what I am made to be; that as a poet I am subject to mood and variation, the highs and lows of experience and temperament. That as a *seeker* of truth rather than a *finder* maybe I'm a kind of pioneer for other questioners, and that I should accept that as my calling. I've even had Christian leaders tell me that my doubts are my "gifts to the church" as challenges to an easy or superficial faith. And I've been able to accept that God isn't offended by my doubts.

I recount to Richard the stories about my sporadic epiphanies—those occasional moments when everything, *everything*, felt whole and holy and vibrating with meaning and beauty. Each time this had happened I had been alone, out of doors, often in a setting of great natural beauty—a wide solitary Caribbean beach, a deep Northwest pine forest, a highway through wide-open country with no other cars in sight, a coastal boat harbor seen through fog and sun like a mystical vision. As if God reached down and touched me with a larger understanding of creation.

Once, reading again the story of Paul's Damascus road conversion, I'd entered his experience like a personal vision. I'd participated in it so deeply that I felt I *was* Paul. In every case I'd tried to hold on to the moment, the experience, recording it in my journal, hoping to make it last. But because by very nature an epiphany is fleeting, the experience had been time-bound, cut back by the normal activity of life.

As Richard (he'd said, "Call me Richard!") hears me out, it comes out that I am a poet, and a devotee of the metaphysical poets, with a special love of the life and writings of Gerard Manley Hopkins. "Oh! So you celebrate *haecceity*!" Richard laughs. We share our understanding and excitement about the concept of "this-ness" or "is-ness"—the essential, unique quality of every created thing, large and small— a concept advanced by fourteenth-century philosopher-theologian John Duns Scotus and much loved by Hopkins, who imaged it forth in his poems with their "inscapes," their celebration of all vivid, created things, spatial or subatomic, everything glowing with intrinsic value. "Glory be to God for dappled things . . . / all trades, their gear and tackle and trim. / All things counter, original, spare, strange; / Whatever is fickle, freckled (who knows how?)"[1]

Richard turns his head and gazes out the dining hall window, focusing on the poplar tree in front of us, its green leaves shimmering in the heat. He tells me, "I could sit for hours and simply contemplate that tree. Those leaves. Even *that* one leaf in particular" (he points). He suggests to me that, when my mind complicates or questions what I believe, I might "choose an object—rock, leaf, a pool of water—for quiet contemplation. When your mind wanders, as it will, return to focusing on what is there in front of you. Let your gaze stay with the awareness that God is in you and in this object, that you are both part of a universe that is an ongoing creation of Love." He calls this "a long, loving look at the real."

I know what he means about the importance inherent in a detail. As a poet such elemental examples speak to me as well. It's the specific detail that captures me and gives the poem hooks to hang on. The individual essence of a color, a shape, a focal point that then propels me into a poem and lends it its authenticity, its sensuousness.

And now I can intuit that every detail is a part of something infinite. Yes. The conversation opens up more ideas, uncovers enlarging connections. We agree that as we continue to learn, quantum physics suggests that physical and incorporeal realities are united in the structure of the universe.

But then, my old, sad internal puzzle finds its way back into the conversation, "If God loves, *really* loves me, why doesn't he let me know in a way I can feel?" Where is God? Who is he?

"Don't let those old contradictions inhabit your heart," he responds. "Doubt is a lack, not a crime. Negativity is a habit to which the immature human heart naturally goes. As you let divine love erode that fear, you'll learn to feel the power of no-ego, that God is in you and you are in God. Learn to make that oneness your way of life." I realize that my old self-importance, desperate for recognition and authentication, has had me in its grip, holding me back from the freedom of giving and receiving love without the barrier of earning approbation. This has been for me a problem even deeper than the cosmological contest between faith and physics.

Richard expands on the theme of Christ the Creator, who holds the whole universe in an ongoing creative generosity in which each individual created thing is born to be a part. He calls this aspect of God "the cosmic Christ," a term I've reacted to negatively in the past, out of the straitjacket of my old theology. But Paul, in Colossians, fills in the details. For Rohr, the creation paradigm illustrates Christ operating way beyond and within the explanatory thrusts of science. God doesn't compete with science. He is its source, its presence and its fulfillment.

And Jesus? The eternal, preexistent Creator Christ became a human body in space and time—the bodily manifestation of this ongoing creatorship within the Trinity, under three modes but one in essence. All and each of them united in displaying limitless bounty. It is Jesus who makes the human connection, linking us with the Father and the Spirit. As "the firstborn over all creation" he has been there since the beginning: "He is before all things, and in him all things hold together. . . . For God was pleased to have all his fullness dwell in him, and through him to reconcile to himself all things, whether things on earth or things in heaven" (Colossians 1:15, 17, 19-20 NIV). The Word became flesh. How could I have not seen the extent of this, its fulfillment in individual believers before?

As Richard and I continue to uncover what has been hindering my intimacy with God, doubts and anxieties fall away. It's like taking the cap off a perfume bottle to release the fragrance. I feel a rush of release and relief. I experience a kind of buoyancy, suffused with light and life in a way I cannot explain, or explain away.

It's as if I've been looking out at the world through a sliding door, its glass streaked with old dust and fingerprints and then, as the door slides open, the freshness and beauty and color of a large and intricate landscape is suddenly right there, with the warm air blowing in my face and blue heaven beaming down. And I am freed to step out into it, to be enfolded and surrounded by its health and brilliance. In the moment I affirm this fragment of George Herbert's poetry: "The man that looks on glass, / on it may stay his eye, / or if he pleaseth, through it pass / and then the heaven espy."[2] I spy heaven. I move freely within it. And today I still live in that open embrace. It still surrounds and frees me.

Later that day I buy Richard's book about Franciscan spirituality, *Eager to Love*, and have him sign it to me. Which he does, graciously. Then I walk back to my little cell with the sun blessing me. I lie on my cot, feeling as though I am resting in a golden hammock. I have been liberated into belief. I am able to pray, to *feel free* to pray without reserve but with a heart bursting with gratitude. I feel like Mary, "full of grace, "as if I'd been imprinted with light, with joy, with something so boundless it defies description.

Long ago, in my early poem-writing days, I'd written a poem titled "Circles," a reflection on the theme of circles. A circle had struck me as such a universal shape, visible almost everywhere to the knowing eye—raindrops, wedding rings, tears, eagle eyes, planets. The final lines of the poem went like this:

the arc of love from God to women and to men
orbiting, goes to him again.
My love, to loving God above
captures me in the round of love.

I surmise that my early, intuitive self had tuned in to this universal mystery long ago, though my rational, theoretical self had failed to immerse itself in the "round" of God's love. And that God found me wandering and bewildered and turned even that circuitous path into a circle back to him.

And now, quite dramatically, I know that the print of grace has been on me all along, though without my discerning it.

God "creates exquisite wild flowers in hidden valleys that no human eye will ever see, just for the joy of it."[3] This is the God whose delight bursts into creation every day, every minute, if we have hearts to welcome it and become part of it. Even my reading of Scripture, my singing of familiar hymns is transformed by the enlarging lens of this wideness and freedom. No longer must I see "through a glass darkly." A new comprehension has taken over.

I no longer have to wonder whether to depend on the belief of my optimistic, faith-filled father or my sour, anxious mother whose doubts and depressions kept her from the fullness of divine love.

Later that summer, as John and I, heading south on our way to visit family, drove through Washington (camping in Oregon), and then crossed into Northern California, my imagination was stirred again into an appreciation of this oneness of creation in its every aspect:

The Haecceity of Travel

With apologies to John Duns Scotus

Anticipating long stretches of nothingness
we plunge south into California on I-5,
prepared to be bored, uninterested in the view,

and a bit worried that we too may
commit monotony. But then, over us, clouds
contribute their lenticular magnitude to
the two-dimensional—carved by winds into
stream-lined eagles or space craft or B-52s.
I take sky photos through the windshield,
admitting that in spite of anonymity, there is never
nothing. Required to obey gravity,
we occupy open space with substance,
all of us on the skin of the planet created
to lift against the earth's pull, yet sustained entirely.
We live out our singularity along with olive and
almond trees, oleanders, tarmac, large trucks,
until size becomes irrelevant: smoke blue coastal range,
stem of dry grass, brittle eucalyptus leaf,
pebble ground into the ground—each bears love's print,
is held, a particulate within the universe.
Even the small, soft moth on the window of
the rest area's dingy washroom, unaware of our scrutiny,
its russet wings traced with intricacies of gray,
owns an intrinsic excellence.

Much later, I was able to write a kind of poetic summary
of my long traveling, an overview of my search for and new
experience of God's truth, beginning with its loneliness and
uncertainty and reaching a place of rest and release:

Suspended

Faith was its own high wire
on which I danced or threaded my way
through what often felt like vast emptiness
strung across a great silence.

Or I was a pair of sneakers
dangling by their dirty laces from the line,
punched by wind. Never quite dislodged.
The *gravity* of the situation. The violent
weave of soul weather. The panic surges.
We know that planes, their trails weaving
the high blue, somehow hang their weight
in space. But I am not a large and
efficient machine, merely a common insect
with the possibility of wings

until I'm lifted, not by an act of will,
not unwillingly either, and with no effort,
but with a deft tenderness, then laid
in a hammock of gold ribbons
strung within the great bowl of
the universe itself. I need no pinions.
In this immensity my minor weight
is upheld, wholly.

nine

Scars and Stains

*O*nce again the winter rains of the Pacific Northwest are here, and as drops begin to fall we see the circles widen and intersect on the surface of a pond, a lake, a puddle. And later in the season, the delicacy of flakes of snow, and the beauty and purity with which they cover the rooftops and fields, are imprints that stay in our visual memories. But they are not scars. Unlike a shattered mirror, the water's surface heals, the flakes thaw and vanish as the weather systems shift.

But what about welts and marks that leave a lasting impression? Throughout the Bible, God's personal attention to individuals is described in different ways. Many of them are marked for specific roles. Presumably Adam, there in the primal garden, bore a healed scar in his side where his rib had been when Eve was lifted from his body in God's original thoracic surgery. It was also a kind of birth; a new human being entered the world in a way never duplicated before or since. Whether we take the creation story in Genesis literally or as what C. S. Lewis called "true myth," the narrative is compelling and informative.

And after the first fratricidal murder, brother on brother, Abel was killed and Cain survived. Cain, afraid that his reputation as a killer would follow him, feared for his life. But God put a protective mark on him as a warning to others not to harm him.

When God entered a covenant relationship with his chosen people—the descendants of Abraham, Isaac and Jacob—he distinguished them as uniquely different. This involved circumcision, a ritual cutting of the male penis at birth that marks Jews for life. This little surgical procedure continues to be practiced around the world, not only by Jewish people, though the health benefits of circumcision continue to be debated. Paul talked about "the circumcision of the heart" for the chosen ones of the new covenant, who comprise the church. Rather than emphasizing a physical, outward sign, Paul commends an inward attitude of heart that conforms us to the likeness of Christ.

Because he questioned the angel who brought him and his wife the birth announcement, Zechariah, father of John the Baptizer, was stamped with muteness until after his child's arrival. His doubt that his wife could bear a child in old age suggested that, for him, God's purpose was an impossibility, much as Abraham had doubted that Sarah, in a similar situation, could produce an heir. Zechariah must have been relieved that his muteness was not permanent, but surely this muteness must have cast a nine-month shadow over his life that would be impossible to forget.

The man born blind was given sight, healed by Jesus. Lazarus and the son of the widow of Nain were both raised from the dead by Jesus with a word. What does it take for such dramatic reversals to occur? Did Jesus' word of healing leave its permanent imprint? It makes us wonder, *How in our day may we speak words of healing and restoration in Christ's name?*

No matter how we protect, care for, or pursue physical or spiritual renewal for ourselves, our life paths imprint us. Though sometimes this is a result of our own choices, at other times we are subject to conditions over which we have little control—diseases, accidents, anomalies. Like it or not, as our years multiply we bear evidence of our experiences as human beings. Our skin loosens and wrinkles, our muscles gradually atrophy, our vision and hearing dim, our memories become less reliable, our circles of community dwindle because of diminishing energy and fatigue.

I can testify to the truth of this! It is too close to home to deny it.

Evening

We lie together on the big bed,
waiting for sleep to take her.

> She burrows into me like a chick
> into feathers, wanting warmth
> no down comforter can offer.
> Under the covers she stretches out a finger —
> her small, firm, probing digit —
> to test the bare skin of my arm,
> feeling its wrinkles like crepe, but soft,
> the way a tired rubber band
> loses the memory of stretching.
> Gram, she wonders aloud, will my skin
> ever get like that? I am her example
> of the way flesh loses itself along with
> muscles, bones, other members, including
> the part that wonders and asks questions
> she hasn't even thought of yet.

No matter how we try to hold on to our youthful appearance or beautify ourselves cosmetically, mortality is a disease without a cure but for the prospect of transition and translation to a new state of being. We believe that Jesus has a body in heaven (witness the nail prints), but will we? Age leaves its irreparable imprint on our bones, our skin, our hearing, our thought patterns. Will our translation into the eternal state remove our freckles and tauten our flesh? We'll have to wait and find out, and by then, most likely, it won't matter!

A recent photo spread of images in a national magazine discussing the Egyptian uprising in Cairo included a full-page view of the back of the young man known as the "Singer of the Revolution" in Tahrir Square, who was tortured for the temerity of his protest. The horrifying crisscross of welts and scars from red-hot iron and electrical burns were indelibly scorched into his flesh. He survived. The scars will heal over—by the magic of cellular restoration—but during his lifetime the scars and memories will never disappear, reminders of this brave individual's sacrifice.

Somehow, each of these scars remind me of the most profound and indelible markings of all—those that Jesus bore from the Roman lashing, and the abrasions on his hands and knees from the stumble onto gravel under the weight of the cross, and then the dreadful, penetrating wounds of the nails and the spear. Later, these unhealed wounds were indubitable proof to Thomas that Jesus had actually risen in the flesh. (Imagine feeling with your fingers into the deep, hot slash in Jesus' torso!) Many biblical scholars believe that those wounds will be visible to us in heaven.

Some of God's saints throughout history have borne the mysterious physical stigmata, the five holy wounds that Jesus had—on hands, feet, side—that survived his death and resurrection and continue to bear witness to his sacrifice. They still bind him to us, linking his deity with our humanity.

My son, who does medical work and public health training

for a humanitarian agency in Thailand and Burma, sent us photos of Ser Ku Paw, a young girl from a village in Karen State in Burma (Myanmar). On a Christmas Day she got too close to the fire on the family hearth, and her polyester T-shirt melted as it burned, clinging to her flesh and resulting in burns so severe that as they healed they left scarring on her upper torso and neck and face so extensive that she could not raise her head or close her mouth or move her arms freely. Ser Ku Paw was eventually evacuated to a hospital in Thailand where, after months of reparative surgery and skin grafts, she gained greater freedom of movement and relief from pain. A great deal of prayer had been offered for her healing. We wonder, though, about the scars in her memory. The Karen people are noted for their resilience and healing from damage, but, we wonder, will this young woman ever be able to overcome the horror of the little holocaust in her own home?

Yes, the miracles of modern medicine, with its cunning technologies and therapies, are restorative. Yet they can only delay the inevitable decline of our mortality that ends in death. Of body. Not of spirit.

I have a thick, visible scar on my right hand left over from the time I was trying to put a scared cat into a carrier for a trip to the vet. It has healed over, but still reminds me of the struggle that resulted in blood from her sharp claws, and my fear of infection. I have surgical scars on my belly, my right and left knees, my left ankle, my first finger on my left hand.

They are the scars of healing rather than torture, replacing arthritic knees and an ankle that was full of spurs and bone chips from my athletic youth. A hip replacement may be next! I am grateful but realistic about the impermanence of my mortal body.

Many of us also have wounds of the soul from the past. Though they are invisible to others, they may continue to affect our outlook on life. Negative criticism, humiliation, disappointment, abuse, estrangement, shame and betrayal in early life may shadow our human spirit, clinging despite our efforts to banish them.

For some, the word *stigma* refers to the shame of some indignity, a dark past of failure or misdeed or crime that is hard to outlive. It is like a branding, an adhesive label or a trap from which they cannot escape. Cain bore the stigma of the murder of his brother Abel for the remainder of his life. God marked him for his protection, but also as a witness to his disobedience and rebellion.

Is it possible to take the concept of stigma, a marking that often suggests shameful behavior, and turn it into an affirmative sign? More than just wearing a cross as a symbol of our affiliation with Christ, can we as sensate, articulate, active children of God be marked, stigmatized, for our love, our patience, our kindness, our openness, our truth telling, our trustworthiness, our compassion? If that kind of stigma could be applied to members of God's human family, it could become a sign, a catalyst for change and renewal in a desperately trapped and struggling world, and turn the word *stigma* into a mark to be desired, not dreaded.

St. Paul wrote about his "thorn in the flesh" (2 Corinthians 12:7 NASB), evidently some physical affliction so aggravating that he entreated God for relief. His request was denied. He'd been writing to his friends in Corinth about what I think of as being "hijacked into paradise" fourteen years earlier (perhaps right after the time of his conversion?), an experience that defied human explanation or description. He couldn't, or wouldn't, discuss it or enlighten them, possibly because he himself wasn't sure if this was a physical or psychological event in which he heard the divine "unspeakable" uttered, evidently some ecstatic revelation that he'd been forbidden to talk about. He admitted that such an experience might well have made him feel superior to others who hadn't been privileged with such a heavenly disclosure.

Paul's Thorn

*"Therefore, to keep me from being conceited, I was given
a thorn in the flesh, a messenger from Satan. . . ." 2 Cor. 12:7*

Thorn — the word meaning
sharpened stake. Even as metaphor
it feels fierce. And simply to keep pride
at bay? It seems a harsh mercy,

this gift sent from God via Satan —
Or was the Father saying, "Paul, this
is what happened to my son, thorns
crown-pressed his forehead.
A stake buried itself in his own side
and spikes pinned his hands and feet
into the pulp of a wooden beam.
When Paul bragged from time to time,
we wonder — where did God pierce him? Tooth?
Armpit? Groin? Naked sole? We speculate,
feeling for him and owning our own shortcomings.
When my bone breaks does it mean I am
conceited, and therefore called
to thank heaven for the infliction? But cancer,
and the baby, born after five failures
taken in his crib at four months. Thorns?
How to make sense of this, and how
to answer our perplexities? I've never
been hi-jacked to the third heaven, yet
may I learn to crop my secret self-
importance as a means towards discipline,
pain a divine endowment. If possible, I'll
put up with that sharp gravel in my sandal;
and a sore that will not heal. I'll ask:
Is it vexation, or disguise for grace?

In his writings Paul had actually shown a fair amount of bravado, outlining his qualifications and experiences in this letter to the Corinthians, perhaps in order to assert his authority as an apostle. Here God's caring love kicked in for Paul, guarding him from the sin of pride. He'd been given some physical disability to keep him from being big-headed, from claiming some kind of superiority or advantage over other believers. Commentators have speculated that it had something to do with his eyesight. Perhaps it was a neurological disorder or an allergy. Paul was enigmatic about it, but he took it seriously. If God wouldn't eliminate it, he realized it must be for his own good.

And stains? I'm thinking of a favorite shirt of my husband's, with its dark marks on the shirt front of indelible ink from the pen he carries in his pockets. He wears it anyway.

Grass stains on a T-shirt. Marks of wear and tear on upholstery. And then I think of a tablecloth in our dining room that still sustains an ugly blot of dark on the fabric, the mark of wax spilled years ago from a lighted candle. Various remedies have been suggested, but none of them works quite well enough. There may be wine stains on a carpet or rust stains in an old bathtub or scaling on a handrail. Unsightly, irritating and indelible.

The stains of past wrongdoings on our conscience and

consciousness are far more troubling because they are interior, and while they may not be visible to others they continue to affect our attitudes and behaviors. Someone may have lived a life of crime and been guilty of abuse or homicide. Even after receiving the appropriate penalty or serving jail time, that reputation clings and causes suspicion that may last a lifetime.

Corrosion happens when acid hits metal. If, about a wrong done to you or someone you love, the acid of bitterness lingers, it will eat away at your soul health.

What resolution is there for the stains of shame and guilt? Forgiveness is the only remedy. Repentance, confession and absolution are the Christian answer. My church offers the "rite of reconciliation" with the invitation of confession in the presence of a priest and the assurance of absolution and forgiveness. It is comforting to hear words of acknowledgment and pardon from a human voice, speaking for God, who is always attentive to our repentance, forever willing to forgive and forget. "As far as the east is from the west, so far has He removed our transgressions from us" (Psalm 103:12 NKJV).

While God's forgiveness for true penitence is guaranteed, human forgiveness may not come so easily. For many of us, ahead lies the difficult task of seeking out the offended one to offer our confession and beg for pardon. We're grateful for the prayer of confession that comes in the liturgy. "Most merciful God, we confess that we have sinned against you in thought, word and deed, by what we have done and by what we have left undone. We have not loved you with our whole heart. We have not loved our neighbors as ourselves. We are truly sorry and we humbly repent. For the sake of your son our Savior Jesus Christ, have mercy on us and forgive us."[1] I pray this in my heart along with the priest every Sunday before Eucharist.

The stain may remain in the minds of others, and we still may have to live with the consequences of our actions.

ten

Marked for Suffering

Job and Jacob

*C*onsider the dramatic story of Job (Job 2:1-10) and the problem of human suffering and vulnerability. C. S. Lewis wrote about this in his books *The Problem of Pain* and, after the death of his wife, *A Grief Observed*, addressing the difficulty we all have in understanding our anguish and mortality—the ongoing elements of our human condition. As Eugene Peterson points out, human suffering is too common, too all-pervasive, for us to complain a lot about it; we've all suffered, perhaps as a result of our poor choices. But it's *undeserved* suffering that really stings, a slow burn that disturbs us.

My husband and I are involved, through our local church, in a ministry to street people in our town—the disadvantaged, the jobless, the homeless, the desperately ill, the mentally unstable. Many are addicted to drugs and alcohol. We meet young women with children hiding from abusive relationships, needing to take cover from a boyfriend or ex-husband. Sometimes, when the safe refuges of women's shelters are full, the victims end up sleeping in their cars, along with their kids and cats or dogs. They run out of gas. Survival from day to day preoccupies them, unable as they are to see beyond this week or this month or to even visualize a future. Some of them camp in the woods, summer and winter, getting their meager provisions from the local food bank and using a big-box store's toilet facilities. We may purchase an inexpensive tent or sleeping bag to shelter them, but severe cold makes life a bitter matter of survival. At intersections they show their cardboard signs: "Homeless. Anything helps. God bless." Walking, trudging, seeking help all over town a day at a time.

We've met young people who want to get an education that would qualify them for a job, but they need the tuition fee for the local community college. With pledges from us and other churches in town we can often help them toward that goal.

Once a week they arrive at our church. We invite them to sit down at a table with us, one by one, our guests, longing to be Jesus to them, to assist in the miracles of change by the power of his Spirit. Their poverty is immediate and unmediated. We are eye to eye, hand to hand with them. There is no mistaking the grime on the skin, the stink of the unwashed, the flush of fever, the glazed eyes of the whacked out. This is no abstraction, no theoretical sociological condition. They are marked indelibly by their deprivation. They want a life for themselves and for their children, but where can it be found? The desperate sense of the impossible overwhelms them. We listen, counsel, pray together, we offer our limited financial resources and referrals. Often our farewell hugs bring tears of emotion or relief.

In any season of economic downturn and uncertainty, we also meet with hard-working citizens who have been laid off from their well-paying jobs—nurses, office managers, teachers, homeowners—their power turned off, facing eviction from their homes, desperate to keep their families together.

It seems so unfair. Our resources seem so inadequate.

The life of Job is an outstanding biblical example of what we might view as unmerited tribulation. He was an influential leader but had resisted the corruption of power. His integrity remained unquestioned. He was a devoted father, interceding daily with God for his seven sons and three daughters. His holdings were more than substantial; and best of all, he worshiped God. This faithfulness got on Satan's nerves; it irritated him.

Here's how the dialogue between God and Satan went, at the beginning of the narrative.

> *The Lord*: "Have you considered my servant Job? There is no one like him on the earth, a blameless and upright man who fears God and turns away from evil?"

Satan: "Oh, come on! That's because he values his health and well-being. But stretch out your hand now, O Mighty One, and strike his bone and his flesh, and then watch how he will curse you to your face!"

The Lord: "Very well, because I trust him, I'll give him into your power, only spare his life."

So Satan followed up on his threats, inflicting "loathsome sores" on Job's body, from the sole of his foot to the top of his head. These lesions were obvious markings, noticeable to all who saw him. They were so bad that Job had to take a broken bit of pottery with which to scrape away the scabs and pus as he sat among the ashes. Still without grumbling at God.

God not only allowed his righteous servant to be marked with a wretched disease but seemed interested in what would happen. We wonder—for what purpose? Why? In effect, Job answers his derisive wife, who urges him to curse God and get it over with, by telling her, "We've taken all the good things in our lives from God, why not the bad?" And in the end, of course, Job's trust in God was rewarded by the return of wealth and the leadership of a large and prosperous family. But he had to do some deep thinking and exhibit ferocious faithfulness to stay the course allotted to him by higher-ups, in the face of "friends" who called themselves comforters but failed to comfort and even added to his trial by accusing him falsely.

Job: Waiting It Out

"How long will you say these things,
and the words of your mouth be a great wind?" — Bildad to Job

Strung on a string between the will of God
and the clutch of Satan, this is pure wretchedness.
You have made a list of tawdry, self-justifying
excuses, but your friend endlessly
considers your statements a mere whine of wind.

He and his allies view you as a specimen
of failure, your body a battlefield of sores and
visible bones, hair matted, eyes wild with looking
to heaven and pleading, pleading for fair judgment.

You are not yet a cadaver available for
forensic investigation, and this is no idle
philosophical discussion with either God or men.
Rather, a prolonged confrontation.

The pious hanker to be proven right
and righteous so they can believe themselves
to be superior. "See? We are not pawns of the powers
like you!" And your body is too weakened

to be energized into coherent response.
Perhaps heaven will transmit answers so
you don't have to. You wait for the harsh words

to die down, for some blessed
silence.

Job was not flawless, but he was faithful even in his despair and
doubt.

His story is full of laments such as this:

Oh, that I knew where I might find [God]. . . .
I go forward, but He is not there,
And backward, but I cannot perceive Him. . . .
But He knows the way that I take;
When He has tested me, I shall come forth as gold. (Job
23:3, 8, 10 NKJV)

Gold is only purified by intense heat in which the metal is
heated to liquidity so that traces of impurity may be skimmed
from the surface. I suspect that many of us, in dark times of
doubt and perplexity, have prayed like Job. He could not have
foreseen any happy ending. Would we have shown such
stalwart faith in similar circumstances? What if we are marked
with unusual suffering that seems unfair, out of proportion to
the life we have led? Job is the kind of exemplar we need to
be reminded of, when through no fault of our own the cir-
cumstances in our lives seem unbearable.

Other biblical characters were marked out among their
contemporaries, and each of the marks had special meaning.
Remember Jacob? The Genesis story gives us many explicit

details of his devious dealings. In spite of his naturally cowardly and manipulative character, God, who is no respecter of persons, picked Jacob out for a special role in the life of the nation to be chosen, as is detailed in Genesis 32.

Jacob had been his mother's favorite and the despair of his father, whom he'd deceived, taking by trickery his brother Esau's inheritance. But later, in one of several dramatic instances, Scripture shows him in a bind. He'd just negotiated a peace contract with his father-in-law, Laban, whom he'd deceived more than once over the years, though he'd ended up marrying two of Laban's daughters. Now he was out of favor with his fraternal rival, Esau, who had good reason to be suspicious of his brother's motives and manners. Jacob was "greatly afraid and distressed," having heard that Esau was on the way to meet him, along with four hundred men—quite a little army.

As was his habit, Jacob set about making plans for his own survival as well as that of his family, servants and possessions, including herds of cattle. By sending off to Esau several successive "gifts" (read: bribes) of flocks and herds of animals, Jacob hoped that in stages he might soften up the brother whose vengeance he feared. He also packed up his family—wives and children—and herded them off to the other side of the river Jabbok for their safety.

Which left Jacob all alone.

Which meant that Yahweh could get at him without his usual defenses.

Out of nowhere, a figure appeared and began an all-night assault on our protagonist. Though the Scripture account describes Jacob's assailant as "a man," Jacob himself soon recognized that this was no ordinary human being. The fierce wrestling match that went on between them until daybreak left him injured, with his hip out of joint, permanently dislocated.

But that wasn't all. You'd think he'd want this aggressor to disappear, to leave him in his exhaustion, giving him a chance to rest and recover. But strangely, Jacob was reluctant for the tussle to end, pleading with the "man" not to leave him without blessing him. TV psychologist Dr. Phil is fond of saying to his guests with problems, "This is going to be a changing day in your life." Jacob must have been desperate enough to long for something different that would release him from a sense of failure in spite of all his human efforts to gain money and power. This was the divine blessing that he received: "I'm changing your name from Jacob to 'Israel,' meaning 'God-Wrestler.' You've wrestled with God, and you didn't give in."

You cannot wrestle anyone at a distance. When engaged in wrestling without spiritual consequences it's just a physical contact sport. But a deep interior grappling with God, involving soul and spirit, may happen at a crisis time and bring about change at some point in our lives.

Jacob called the place of struggle Peniel ("God's face") because, he said, "I have seen God face to face, and my life is

preserved" (Genesis 32:30 NKJV). The Hebrew word for
Yahweh used here translates "The Fear." We too have a God
to be feared and grappled with, perhaps at a low point in our
lives when we have had to summon all our energy in our
confrontation with the divine. No half measures will do. No
lukewarm response. In the face of our desperation God may
reach into us so powerfully that he will leave his stamp, his
print on us, giving us a new name that marks us both to our-
selves and those who know us. I've had experiences like that—
painful, but in the end strengthening and affirming. (This
pivotal story in biblical history marks Jewish diet even today;
some Jews, when ingesting meat, abstain from eating the
thigh muscle. Before it is sold for food, kosher meat has this
muscle extracted as a remembrance of Jacob's hip wound and
his encounter with the Almighty.)

Perhaps the real significance of Jacob's limp and name
change was that God can take someone of doubtful character
and, in the lengthy wrestling match (a pretty flesh-to-flesh
and soul-to-soul tussle and embrace that results in a life-
changing contact), bring about a change of character, leaving
behind a conspicuous mark as a reminder. This gives hope to
all of us, well aware as we may be of our own flaws and failings.
In serious grappling with God in our crises, doubts and fears,
we may come away marked as God's own intimates and heirs.

Some of God's saints have borne the mysterious physical
stigmata, the five holy wounds that Jesus had—on hands, feet,

side, head—that survived his death and resurrection and continue to bear witness to his sacrifice. Such imprints still bind him to us, linking his deity with our humanity.

Naming leaves its special distinctive. In the Old Testament, a name might also confer a blessing or prophecy. Many parents in our time name their children with some reference to an event, or an ideal, or a loving grandparent or friend in hopes that their offspring will live up to their dreams for them. Some memorialize a rising and popular politician or national leader. What name or designation do we want from God?

Then there are the stories of Moses and his sister Miriam leading their nation out of Egypt and across the wilderness. Each of them bore significant emblems of their encounters with God—one negative, the other positive. Miriam was marked with leprosy for her doubt and disobedience in challenging her brother and was excluded from the Israeli camp for seven days (Numbers 12:10). But the story of Moses' meeting with God recorded in Exodus 19 is perhaps the most dramatic in all of Scripture, full of fire, clouds, thunder and piercing trumpet blasts. Mt. Sinai itself shook violently as Yahweh descended upon it, shielded in thick smoke from the gathered people waiting at the mountain's foot. Imagine Moses' apprehension as he obeyed the command to climb the mountain to meet the Mighty One.

The exodus account is followed by chapters of detailed instructions to govern the lives of the Israelites as they approached and settled in the Promised Land. This was followed by more directives to do with the architecture and accouterments of the tabernacle that God was designing as a place of worship, a moveable tent as they progressed across the desert. Even the details of the priests' clothing were pre-arranged, as well as the kinds of animal sacrifices to be offered on the tabernacle's altar.

After all these God-dictated comprehensive directives, the writer of Exodus presents the most dramatic imprint of God's standards for human behavior, the Decalogue, or Ten Commandments. "Moses turned and went down from the mountain, carrying the two tablets of the covenant in his hands, tablets that were written on both sides, written on the front and on the back. The tablets were the work of God, and the writing was the writing of God, engraved upon the tablets" (Exodus 32:15-16). Though Moses later dropped and broke these tablets in outrage at the people's golden-calf idolatry while he was on the mountain, in divine mercy, God provided a second, identical set of his requirements. Those standards remain with us today.

We learn later, in 2 Corinthians, that God marked Moses in a spectacular way (2 Corinthians 3:7). Being with the Almighty left a kind of radiance that lingered on his features even after he returned to the people gathered below. He had to cover his face, shielding the people in the encampment on the desert from its brilliance, except when he visited God in the Holiest Place in the Tabernacle.

My own father, an ardent follower of Christ, himself from a large family of missionaries, exhibited something similar. When he was at home, we would often have gatherings of missionaries or Christian friends in our living room. Sometimes on such occasions I'd notice that Dad seemed to be somewhere else, somewhere transcendent, his face uplifted and shining, lit, it seemed, by the consciousness of divine presence. It looked, it felt, like God's glory manifested.

As a young doctor in Sydney, before serving for many years in the Solomon Islands, he'd had a revelatory experience of the Holy Spirit (this was long before the charismatic renewal that galvanized faith communities later in the century). Many years afterward, as a former missionary surgeon, he spent his time writing and traveling, becoming an international devotional speaker. Every morning in his later years he would rise early, around 4:00 a.m. and "pray his way around the world," mentioning before God the friends and ministries he'd been in touch with, interceding for those with specific needs. He had a rather amazing record of praying for friends who had been trying, unsuccessfully, to conceive a child. On following visits he was often greeted by proud and thankful new parents, asking him to dedicate their newborns to God's service.

Suffering and glory are often linked in the Bible. Paul, in

Romans, tells us "the sufferings of this present time are not worth comparing with the glory about to be revealed to us. For the creation waits . . . " (Romans 8:18-19). And the contrast between the depth of suffering and the ultimate reward of glory heightens the significance of both. If God has allowed us to experience a long night of pain, we may consider it a presentiment of the light of a new day, when our darkness and trouble will be forgotten, subsumed in glory.

eleven

A Sad, Smeared Print

*K*neeling, repentant, we repeat the confession of sin at church every Sunday, telling God we are aware of our sins of commission and omission, preparing ourselves for forgiveness and readiness to eat and drink, partaking of the Eucharist at the holy table. As we kneel and open ourselves to ourselves and God, a few of the words we say together from the prayer book go like this: "Most merciful God, heavenly Father, we confess that we have sinned against you . . . by what we have done and by what we have left undone. . . . We have not loved our neighbors as ourselves. We are truly sorry and we humbly repent."[1] This is known as a collect, in which we in the congregation collectively pray together. But as we pray we search our individual hearts, our thoughts, motives and actions, and send our longing for forgiveness heavenward.

I will call her Linda Gray.

We met after the morning worship service at our annual

parish church picnic. It's held in a local park and was, as always, a generous potluck meal—chicken barbecuing on the grill, casseroles, potato salad, fruit plates and pies. It was a glorious day, with sunshine and the smell of newly cut grass drifting from the golf course nearby. Most of the church family pic-nickers were busily socializing under the group shelter, but the picnic tables extended beyond it, down the hill toward Lake Padden. She was sitting alone, intent on eating, at the furthest end of the line of tables.

The sermon that morning had had something to do with helping others and reaching out to people less fortunate than ourselves. Since most of us in the congregation feel pretty fortunate, this seemed more like theory than practicality. Sure, our church community has an international missions outreach. We contribute to the local food bank and visit parishioners in the hospital after their surgeries and take Communion to the homes of those who are sick or disabled and unable to make it to church on Sundays. But this was in the days before our alms ministry was organized, when we hadn't thought deeply about people unlike us, without jobs or living in the street, or those in thrall to drugs or alcohol. We knew theoretically about the children of homes torn apart by violence and ne-glect. Their needs feel real but too often remote from us, beyond our reach. Almost hypothetical. We were only just beginning to know of our need to develop a greater awareness.

So the sight of this woman sitting alone felt like viewing a strange country through binoculars. Perhaps it was a contemporary parable of Jesus. But it also felt a bit viral, as though if we got too close she might be contagious.

I am easily infected by guilt, and the reference to infection is no exaggeration. It's like an abscess that doesn't heal. I feel compassion without great effort, but failing to act on it becomes one of those sins of omission that continually afflict my conscience. *Compassion* literally means "suffering with." That Sunday afternoon I felt sorry about the loneliness of this woman, sitting solitary at her picnic table. And this time, with the challenge of the sermon ringing in my ears, I felt compelled to do something.

Impulsively I walked down to her table with my own paper plate of food, and after I'd asked if I could eat my meal with her, I sat on the wooden seat next to her and started a conversation. (This sort of thing has never been easy for me, an introvert, but I wanted to be obedient to what seemed to be urging me.)

She told me her full name, but made it clear she wanted people to call her Miss Gray. Mentally, I assumed she was holding on to the fragment of dignity that a proper name implies. A large woman, she seemed mountainous. It was a warmish day, with bright sunshine. (As long as it's not raining and blowing, we call it a good day in Bellingham.) I guessed she was wearing all the garments she owned, topped by an enormous man's overcoat. Like steam rising from a roof after rain, the odor of skin that needs washing suffused the air around her.

We talked. She seemed intelligent and articulate. She had been sleeping on park benches and in bus-stop shelters, but was worried about the cold coming on next winter. She admitted she felt vulnerable. There were predators out there.

"Where's your home?"

"Oregon. I'm just waiting for my family to send me a bus ticket home. But my heavenly Father will take care of me."

So, she was a believer. We had something in common. I was encouraged. An idea started to form.

"Would you like some more lunch? This salad is really good."

I went back to the food table and, wanting to take reasonable precautions, found my pastor. He didn't think she'd be dangerous, but suggested I stay in touch with him. Back at table with Miss Gray I said, "I've got an idea. Would you be interested in coming home with me? We could have some dinner together, and you'd have a safe place for the night." (I also thought a good bath and a change of clothes would be a fine idea.)

She was worried about her belongings; she'd left them hidden behind an abandoned house in town. No problem, I told her. I could pick them up in my station wagon.

That turned out to be challenging. She had fifteen large plastic garbage bags bursting with everything she owned. We piled them into the car, which began to take on the same sneaky odor of decay. She and her goods were closely related.

Back at home, I settled her in our guest room, showed her the bathroom and prepared dinner. She ate rapidly, as if she were intent on filling an enormous void. The word *shoveling* came to mind, and I tried to dismiss it. I hoped to keep an open mind, to discover what immediate needs she had that I might be able to fulfill.

That evening over dinner we talked at length. She was reluctant to reveal much about her background or how she found herself in Bellingham, homeless and destitute. Though she was articulate and seemingly well educated, I began to see hints that Miss Gray was somewhat delusional. "I'm just waiting for my family to send me a bus ticket home." So where was home? "Oh, way south of here." Nothing specific. Would she like me to call her family? "No, no. I'm trusting my heavenly Father to take care of me." Her faith in her heavenly Father seemed boundless, but clearly she was counting on the heavenly Father to compel his earthly children to come to her assistance. I suggested she contact our local YWCA, where women can stay safely, if temporarily. Or the local Lighthouse Mission. Or the Salvation Army. "No. I wouldn't lower myself to be with that scum." She said she didn't want charity from anyone, not even disability or social security. She had no ID; her heavenly Father knew who she was.

I sighed in frustration. Okay. But I showed her the washer and dryer and where the detergent was. "How about us doing some of your laundry? I could start it while you take a shower." She was insulted. "I'm not undressing. I need my privacy." She was clear about the terms attached to any help she might receive. I began to wonder if I'd bitten off more than I could chew.

All that night, even knowing that she was sleeping in the guest room two floors below, I was anxious and perplexed. "God, what have I done? How is this going to play out? What do I do next?" I prayed, asking for wisdom.

In the morning I went down to the guest room and tapped on the door. It was locked from inside. There was no response to my knocking and calling. My husband, who up until then had not been involved, tried the same thing without success; maybe a man's voice had more authority. But no. No response.

Around 10:00 a.m. I reluctantly resorted to greater pressure. "Linda, I have some breakfast for you. And coffee's on." An hour later with no sign of Miss Gray I spoke more firmly. "If you don't come out and let me drive you back downtown, I'll have to call the police." That brought an unwilling response, a mumbled, "Okay." Half an hour later the door opened and out she came, angry, stinky and unrepentant. She had not used the laundry. She was still heavily layered, wearing all the clothes she owned.

Because she was heavy, lame and reluctant to move, I had to support her massive body from behind as we moved upstairs to the main floor and out to the garage.

Her belongings, all fifteen white garbage bags full, were still reeking in my station wagon. I dropped them and their owner off near our church, under the large tree that leaned over her favorite park bench overlooking Bellingham Bay. I felt relieved. I'd done my best, and finally I'd ridden myself of a difficult problem, though her intransigence felt like my failure. I hoped that would be the end of it, that I'd done something at least minimally helpful—that I'd showed compassion in Christ's name.

Two mornings later, at 5:30 a.m., I was wakened by the phone. "Mrs. Shaw, I need you to come pick me up and drive me to Goodwill. I need more clothes. Warmer ones." I responded that I'd be willing to do it this once, and that that would be the end of it.

But it wasn't. The early calls from a downtown pay phone continued sporadically. Though the stink from her plastic bags gradually faded away from the back of my car, the image and impact of her on my emotions did not. As the weather cooled and the nights grew long, she moved herself and her garbage bags to the walkway under our church portico where she was minimally sheltered from the rain and wind. The people in our loving and caring congregation invited her to come into our worship services, where she was loud and disruptive, calling on her heavenly Father on and off during the liturgy. For a month or two she stuck around the church, using the women's restroom as her retreat, locking herself in for hours at a time, which meant locking everyone else out.

We called around the city to all the social service centers we knew—the YWCA, the Salvation Army, the Baptist Church, the Methodist Church, Catholic charities—all of them, wanting to know if they could help. Everyone had the same story. They knew all about her. She'd been moving from church to church in Bellingham for seven years, and we understood that the idea of a family "down south" had been a convenient fiction, a fantasy that she could use to convince herself she belonged to someone, that she was wanted. Or at least to establish an identity to present to a skeptical world. If there was real family somewhere, we guessed they hoped they'd gotten rid of her. And no wonder, we thought. We were, I guess, feeling "compassion fatigue."

After several months of conflict our rector composed a formal letter to Miss Linda Gray, informing her, with regret, that we could no longer permit her to use our church property as her dwelling place. We gave her the address of a local counseling center so that some professionals might assess her mental condition and help her with some decisions about her life and future. She didn't want to listen. We read the letter to her, standing by the front door of the church, and had her read it back to us so we'd be sure she understood it. She was furious. She and her bags were gone that afternoon.

It felt like failure. It was failure, an impasse. We asked ourselves if we had left any imprint of Christ's love on her life. (Oh, God of loving compassion and tender mercy, what could we have done differently? What would Jesus have done?)

What did I learn from this misguided attempt at personal outreach? I still feel the sting of inadequacy in memory. It took a painful wake-up call to discern the difference between the fantasy of being heroic and the gritty reality of flunking the test. My tendency to prove myself, to demonstrate my ability and to feel gratified when I succeeded required a severe correction. I needed the wisdom to know that I was not equipped on my own to handle someone with massive, lifelong problems. For me to attempt such a rescue was evidence of hubris. It's a fine thing to respond enthusiastically when God calls us to help the helpless, but I needed the correction of prolonged distress to remind myself of my personal inadequacy in such a task. Wisdom is sometimes learned only through the experience of failure.

In hindsight it is clear to me that it would take skill and professional experience and community to reach out to her and to the other unfortunates who wander just beyond the fringes of our more "ordinary" lives. And that community is more powerful and trustworthy than individuality.

How interesting that the word *ordinary* harks back to its origin in the idea of order—that which has come to be a pattern of an organized, responsible and predictable behavior. And yet it was Jesus who constantly ministered to those with the most dis-ordered of lives—Zacchaeus, Levi, Judas, lepers, skeptics. This was pure grace at work, leaving an imprint of beauty and healing on the crooked, the ugly, the spoiled.

twelve

God-Printed People

*I*f the previous chapter was a profile of frustration and failure, I profoundly hope to balance it with portraits of some people who have left a vibrant, lasting impression on my little life.

When I was eleven my parents moved the family from Australia to Canada. After leaving his missionary work in the Solomon Islands, my Dad was in demand as an international Christian speaker. We had lived in England and Australia, and this move meant that at a vulnerable time in my life I was leaving behind friends and starting over in a new country, a new culture. I was lonely and off-kilter with the educational systems of this new nation, having just finished a school year in Sydney before diving into the middle of a school year in Toronto. And eighteen months later we shifted back to Australia with similar results. As a result, I got lost in the tangled wilderness of things like algebra, never having learned the fundamentals. I never did!

That first summer in Canada, in the 1940s, my parents sent me off to summer camp in Muskoka. I didn't have the right clothes for camping. My conservative mother did not approve of shorts, and I was the only camp child in a dress. Just one dress! My counselor was kind, but I was too "different" from my campmates to blend in (my accent had an odd British-Australian flavor as well).

But it was at Pioneer Camp in Ontario that the loving imprint of God's grace came in the person of Cathie Nicoll, the camp director (known as Nikky by everyone, campers and counselors alike), a warm, enthusiastic woman of vast leadership experience with Canadian young people. She was the daughter of missionaries to China, but her mission field was set in the campus of Ontario forests and lakes. (Later in her life she was awarded the Governor General's Medal for the imprint she made on thousands of Canadian youth.) And she imprinted me. Her sunny nature and infectious smile partook of the beauty of the camp surroundings, its woods and lakes, and reflected it back on all the youngsters at Pioneer Camp.

When I experimented with cutting my bangs back until they resembled a kind of toothbrush at the top of my brow, Cathie protected me from my mother's wrath. (But she never let me forget the anxiety she felt about what Mother would say when my parents showed up to drive me home from camp!) She was musical, funny and genuine in her generous friendships. Over a long and fruitful life she became our hero, inspiring young women in their formative years, many of whom ended up on the frontlines of Christian ministry and leadership.

Ontario Pioneer Camp, where I spent many summers, was and still is on Lake Clearwater in Muskoka, seventy miles or so north of Toronto. I remember its mossy green shores, its six-person tents on raised wooden platforms mounted among the trees overlooking the water. I remember its cool mornings when we would shiver our way down to the lakefront and take an early dip, with washcloths and Ivory soap that floated when it slipped from our hands. Each of our tents had a name and we would all compete for the neatness trophy after morning checkup. It was at Pioneer that I learned to canoe, swim and dive. When I bought my first canoe paddle, Cathie ("Nikky") painted my name on the blade in bold Old English script. More than seventy years on, I still have good biceps from canoeing! I'm imprinted with a canoeing song that helped the paddlers to work in sync: "My paddle's clean and bright / flashing like silver / swift as the wild goose flight / dip, dip and swing!"

I was a flaky, immature youngster, out of touch with North American culture after moving from Australia. But I began to grow, summer by summer, in responsibility and confidence. A few years later, as a teen, I helped lead canoe trips along chains of lakes around Huntsville, Ontario. My love of nature and wilderness was born in those summer camping weeks.

Cathie Nicoll urged us all toward fullness of life, taking risks, trying new things. It was Cathie who applauded the loudest when I learned to do a flawless back dive from a springboard. And at Pioneer I earned a Red Cross lifesavers' certificate that required some strenuous swimming while towing a disabled swimmer to safety.

Many, many years later I was invited to speak at a large Christian women's conference in Calgary, and there was Cathie on the platform to introduce me! I felt deeply honored and humbled and somewhat incredulous that this sterling, loving, beautiful woman could now speak well of me, her erstwhile adolescent, when it was she who had guided and cheered me on.

All of us may have had family, friends or colleagues who influenced us for good. Or not. But some stand out, particularly at change points or times of growth and transition. One shining, never-to-be-forgotten star on my young-adult horizon was Dr. Clyde S. Kilby, a professor of English at Wheaton College and later its department head.

After my high school graduation in Toronto my parents urged me to go to Wheaton because of its reputation as a Christian college. Their dream was for me to be, like them, a foreign missionary, and they thought a Christian education/anthropology concentration would help prepare me for work overseas.

I did my best and had no trouble academically, but found the education courses dry and uninspiring. I tried out a couple of other majors, but when I took an English literature course (a requirement) my whole life trajectory shifted. The course, on the metaphysical poets, was taught by Dr. Kilby, and Donne, Herbert, Vaughn, Crashaw and Hopkins became the focus of my concentration. I felt immediately at home in this world of language and literature, interpretation, debate, and entry into the poetic intelligence evidenced in their lives and literature. It was like diving into a pool of bracing possibilities and learning to swim with assurance. I signed on for more courses—Shakespeare, the Romantics, contemporary poets, anything taught by this brilliant but unassuming Southern professor and other teachers in the English faculty: Leland Ryken, Beatrice Batson, Joe McClatchey, Paul Bechtel.

This was not the direction my parents had envisaged. In my sophomore year my dad flew down to Wheaton from Toronto and challenged my mentor. "Dr. Kilby, I'm appealing to you. Please don't interfere with my daughter's missionary vision," he began. Benign and courteous but firm, my teacher responded, "Dr. Deck, excuse me, but I believe that's *your* vision, not your daughter's." Perhaps Dad had wondered if this might happen. Saving souls as a missionary surgeon in the Solomon Islands had always been his highest ambition, but he'd always encouraged my elementary-school-girl efforts at poetry, carrying around in his briefcase copies of my early verses to show to friends. I was hugely relieved when, with grace and perhaps new insight, Dad backed down, and from then on I flourished in the English Department.

Clyde and Martha Kilby had no children, and generations of English lit students became their kids. I think I became one of the Kilbys' special projects, and with other students I would meet for weekly seminars in the Kilby home. Sometimes I would show up at their second-floor apartment early mornings and find Clyde answering letters. (His practice was to answer on the next day every letter he received, following the practice of his own hero, C. S. Lewis.) He spent those mornings in his pajamas writing in an easy chair in the glassed-in porch, the same porch where he experimented with keeping plants alive in winter. He encouraged not only his English lit students but pots of irises and even dandelions, in a row along the sunny windowsill, which we all found hilarious and charming. Maybe he thought of me as a young dandelion in whom he saw the promise of flowers.

He was always happy to connect with my existential questions and provide a willing sounding board for my new writing and thinking. It was under his tutelage that I learned and experienced the power of the imagination and metaphor to explore life's wide and varied landscapes. It was he who pointed out to me that at least a third of the Bible is in the form of poetry. Under his mentoring, my mind expanded and opened like a seedpod.

Once, as a sophomore, I was given the assignment of a research paper on the Romantic poets—William Wordsworth in particular. I felt the pull of Wordsworth's reflections on nature, and it catapulted me into a new, lengthy poem of my own, about green and growth as a kind of symbol of the soul. When I handed it in instead of the assigned paper, Dr. Kilby gave me an A+ and noted on my paper in red ink, "Send this to *The Atlantic* tomorrow!" Such rule-breaking encouragement gave me the impetus I needed. I began to write freely and contribute to the college literary magazine, later becoming its assistant editor. After graduation (and, five days later, my wedding to Harold Shaw), we moved near enough to Wheaton to continue our close friendship with the Kilbys. He and Martha were family, joining us for Thanksgiving dinners for many years. At these events he would invariably stand in front of the refrigerator and engage in literary conversations while I was trying to make dinner! We walked with them every spring among the daffodils in the Morton Arboretum nearby, thinking about Wordsworth.

Not a poet himself but a lover of poetry, Clyde was a very discerning critic. I continued to send him sheaves of my poems and receive them back, marked up with his distinctive red pencil notes, comments, suggestions and encouragements. I am a writer today largely because of his advocacy in those early years of my writing life.

As a graduate and a young married woman living with my family in nearby in West Chicago, I was often able to drop by the English Department office at Wheaton. This was in the fifties, when C. S. Lewis's writings were just beginning to attract a wide audience in the United States. Clyde Kilby was an early enthusiast. He corresponded with Lewis and was significantly responsible for spreading the word about the British writer and his colleagues in North America. In 1976, after my husband Harold and I had started our own independent publishing company, we published a book, *Tolkien and the Silmarillion*, that tells the story of the summer Clyde spent with an aging J. R. R. Tolkien, encouraging him, albeit unsuccessfully, to complete the epic myth begun with *The Lord of the Rings* trilogy.

Through Clyde we at our young publishing house came into possession of a first edition of *The Pilgrim's Regress* with Lewis's own underlinings and annotations in the margins. I remember wondering, did Lewis, like many authors, read over his published book to hunt for typos, or to question his early interpretations of culture, history and faith? The book has now been reprinted in a beautiful large format by Eerdmans Publishers so that Lewis's emendations give us a clearer path to his later thinking.

After Lewis's death in 1963, Clyde was able to requisition some of Lewis's belongings, and those of other Inklings such as J. R. R. Tolkien, that were being auctioned off. (I could have had the family cat, but I couldn't condemn the feline in question to the six-month quarantine required before its entry into the States.) When the Lewis family wardrobe arrived at Wheaton in a large shipping crate transported all the way from the Kilns in Headington, Oxfordshire, we were intrigued by the fact that upon opening the wardrobe door (it felt as if we were entering Narnia) we discovered that a large, tweedy, charcoal-black "greatcoat" was still hanging in it. With breathless anticipation we plunged our hands into the deep pockets in hopes of discovering some recognizable Lewis memorabilia. Maybe a tuft of Aslan fur? Or the dottle of ash from a pipe? Though all we found was some lint and a bent paper clip, the wardrobe became a symbol of all the writings and artifacts that arrived with Lewis and his six Inklings friends, whose works make up the Marion E. Wade Collection, a study and resource center in Wheaton that is visited by scholars from all over the world.

After the Kilbys retired and returned to their home in Columbus, Mississippi, we were able to stay in close touch with both of them by phone and letter. I continued to send Clyde poems and keep our written conversations going. Martha sent me recipes and crocheted potholders (that I still use). Like many of his former students and their families, we considered them the honorary grandparents to our children. My youngest daughter, Kristin, has Kilby as her middle name. And Clyde left her his teacart, which I rescued from Wheaton several years ago, driving cross-country from Bellingham and back delivering this keepsake to my daughter.

One evening, after talking on the phone to Martha in Mississippi, I asked if Clyde was around. "Oh, he's out on the garden working on his irises. Wait, I'll get him." He came to the phone and for a while we talked affectionately about his life and mine, and just before saying goodbye he said, "Always remember, you are a true poet. I love you." Next morning a friend called to let me know that in the night he had died in his sleep. Perhaps I was the last friend to talk with him, and ever since his parting words have been like a banner flying over my own writing and living.

Wheaton's Marion E. Wade Center, first established by Kilby as the C. S. Lewis Collection, is now a center for international study of Lewis and his colleagues and friends, writers like Tolkien, G. K. Chesterton, Charles Williams, Owen Barfield, George MacDonald, Dorothy Sayers. And Wheaton College's English Department has established the Clyde S. Kilby chair in his honor.

Many friends and colleagues look back at his tenure, his teaching, his example and influence as transformative, none more than me. By simply being himself, honest, humble, warm, a scholar, a friend full of grace, Clyde Kilby contributed to the kingdom of God in ways that generations of students still applaud looking back on with gratitude.

And then there was Madeleine L'Engle, my longtime soul friend. We first met and immediately connected at a Language and Literature conference at Wheaton around 1977 where we were both speakers. I've written at length about our friendship elsewhere, but here are some of the highlights.

We worked as author (Madeleine) and editor (me) on eleven of her manuscripts, beginning with *Walking on Water*. After we'd first published a book of her poetry, *The Weather of the Heart*, I'd suggested she record her thoughts about the companionship of art and faith (she was a liberal, left-leaning Episcopalian; I was a conservative, right-leaning evangelical). Somehow, in the grace of God, we met in the middle, learning much from each other, influencing each other and being enriched in the process. Several months later she handed me a large and untidy sheaf of typescript, declaring, "Can you *do* something with this? It has no *shape!*" I managed to sort through it and rearrange it in little paper piles on my living-room floor that formed more coherent chapters. She and Hugh, her actor husband, loved the result. I published it as *Walking on Water*, and from then on Shaw Publishers became her publisher for her "religious" books—eleven of them over the years.

We visited often back and forth between the Midwest and New York. Later, our husbands, Hugh and Harold, both died of cancer the same year, and we mourned together cross-continent on the phone. Madeleine rescued me from depression more than once, talking me down over the phone. And after she had grave injuries from a car accident in Los Angeles, I flew down and kept her company for a couple of weeks, spending time daily in her hospital room. We told each other stories, told jokes (M. had a vast repertoire), wrote poems together as she healed.

We spent a lot of time together at Crosswicks, her country home in Goshen, Connecticut, driving north from Manhattan. Afternoons we'd go out driving in the country, the Litchfield hills. She'd say, "Let's take the first right turn, then the first left-hand turn and so on and see where we end up." This felt a bit risky. What if I got Madeleine L'Engle lost somewhere in the boonies? On my visits to her condominium on New York's Upper East Side we would walk together to the Cathedral of St. John the Divine on Amsterdam Avenue for noon prayer. She had an office on the grounds as librarian to the cathedral. I would give her earrings and winter hats, which she always wore when we got together. She gave me many gifts, most of them carvings or images of angels from the cathedral gift shop. (I was accumulating a lot of odd-shaped angels. When she thought my home office was looking too holy, she gave me a gargoyle to even things out.)

Our birthdays were ten years and one month apart. One year I asked what she'd like for hers. She said, "Go on a trip with me." So we visited England, Scotland and Ireland with out mutual friend Barbara (the three of us had what we called a trinitarian friendship), me driving since I'd had experience with a right-hand drive. We made up rowdy and sometimes raunchy limericks as we drove. Madeleine's frequent remark as we followed narrow, winding country roads bordered by high hedges was, "Leftish, Luci. Leftish." It seemed like a theological directive.

I also drove Madeleine from Bellingham up through the Canadian Rockies. Sometimes conversation would lag a bit, and I knew M. was pondering an idea for a book. She always had a book going in her head and kept her ideas recorded in her daybook. This was also my habit.

Years later Barbara and I sat together with her in a hospital room as her son, Bion, died of cancer. Watching his last breaths. Praying for his soul. Such experiences knit us in companionship, in the realities of life and death

As her energy and memory grew unreliable in later years, she moved into a nursing home in Litchfield. In the fall of 2008 I flew out from Bellingham to see her, joined by Barbara. She didn't know us. She seemed locked into herself. We sang a hymn together and her face brightened briefly. We left some photos of our times together for her to see. As we left, I asked the receptionist at the front desk to call me if she woke from her inner self. A month later she did, and we talked animatedly for about twenty minutes by phone. She told me, "We should be playing Scrabble!"

On my return home I wrote this poem:

To the Edge

for Madeleine L'Engle

Be with her now. She faces the ocean
of unknowing, losing the sense
of what her life has been, and soon

will be no longer as she knew it, as
we knew it with her. Lagging behind,
we cannot join her on this nameless shore.

Knots in her bones, flesh flaccid, the skin
like paper, pigment gathering like ashes driven
by a random wind, a heart

that may still sing, interiorly — we cannot
know — have pulled her far ahead of us,
our pioneer.

As we embrace her, her inner eyes embrace
the universe. She recognizes heaven with its
innumerable stars — but not our faces.

Be with her now, as you have
sometimes been — a flare that blazes,
then dulls, leaving only a bright

blur in the memory. Hold her
in the mystery that no one can describe
but Lazarus, though he was dumb

and didn't speak of it. Fog has rolled in,
erasing definition at the edge. Walking
to meet it, she hopes soon to see

where the shore ends. She listens as
the ocean breathes in and out in waves.
She hears no other sound.[1]

In September we learned that she had died. Her books live
on. Our memories of her thrive.

Conclusion

*S*ome markings are more permanent than others, carved in stone like the words and emblems on gravestones and the names or sayings on church pillars and the entrance to government buildings. Some are transitory—the patterns of drops on a rain-pocked beach, footprints in the mud, leaves floating on the surface of a stream. Even the mark of ashes on our foreheads on Ash Wednesday, a reminder of our mortality, will be washed away by the following day.

The devastating marks in the forest of wreckage by storm will take longer to be grown over again with new green life, as will the blaze marks left on the trees along a wilderness trail.

Some of us have crosses tattooed on our skin in ink that will not fade—marks of identity. We may wear a cross around our neck as a reminder to ourselves and others that we serve the Christ who made that cross memorable, earth-changing. Even glitzy crosses worn casually as a kind of jeweled statement may still send a message to those who search for meaning: "This symbol has significance beyond itself."

Grace and wisdom come to us in flashes of intuition, even in the things our hands are making, the attitudes and actions that show our personal growth in lives that God is continually reshaping, remaking. Jeremiah tells us,

> I went down to the potter's house, and there he was working at his wheel. The vessel he was making of clay was spoiled in the potter's hand, and he reworked it into another vessel as seemed good to him.
>
> Then the word of the LORD came to me: Can I not do with you, O house of Israel, just as this potter has done? says the Lord. Just like the clay in the potter's hand, so are you in my hand, O house of Israel. (Jeremiah 18:3-6)

Here's a poem by Dr. Randy White, written as a prayer of intention for a friend and sent to me as part of a manuscript he was writing, about poems designed to be used as intercessory prayers:

Potter God

Potter God, who whirled the wheel with your left foot,
Who spun the table with the lump of my friend on top,
Who smoothed the edges with your palms gliding upward
And thinned the sides with the arc of your hand
As he rose in height and took form —
My friend, oozing through your fingers as you pressed,

My friend, collapsing and buckling at points
Then being remade according to your fancy—
Potter God, you who left your swirling prints in his softness,
Made them permanent in the firing
Potter God, who lets this vessel be used in this careless world,
Not protected behind glass on some celestial shelf,
But filled and placed precariously to be
Jostled, chipped, cracked, worn, weathered
Repair him. Re-fill him.
Raise him in tribute.

Acknowledgments

I have been pursuing the torturous conception and growth of this baby for many years, sometimes forgetting and almost aborting it by neglect. It first showed its embryonic self as an idea for a plenary address at the Calvin Festival of Faith and Writing (and here I give grateful acknowledgment to my faithful friend Barbara Braver, who suggested the idea of a thumbprint as a divine marking on our planet and our individual lives). The address was delivered and then the text almost forgotten. Thereafter, like an unborn child, it somehow survived in the womb of an old laptop.

Needing material to practice on, I later resurrected it for workshopping spiritual writing at The Glen Workshop under Paula Houston's skillful and encouraging coaching. There I amplified it a bit, but then shelved it again as other pressures and projects took over.

Years passed. At another Glen Workshop in Mount Holyoke, Massachusetts, I rediscovered the text in my laptop, read it over and wondered, *Is there something usable here? Might it still come to life? And if so, what should I do to nourish and deepen and strengthen it?*

It was then the unborn but tenacious thumbprint theme began again to take over. New ideas and images arrived, demanding to be attended to. And once again, The Glen Workshop was the setting not only for the source of growth in the writing but for my thinking and being and believing. There, in Santa Fe, New Mexico, I met Fr. Richard Rohr, the Glen chaplain that year, who with his wisdom and vision turned my spiritual life inside out and upside down. I knew I had to make this writing the centerpiece, the birth announcement of my spiritual liberation and purpose in God. And in each case it was because Greg Wolfe and the *Image* staff have made The Glen Workshops a vital part of their vision and outreach. And I was the beneficiary.

My agent, Kathryn Helmers, urged me to send the emerging book to InterVarsity Press, where I feel very much at home and where Cindy Bunch, editor extraordinaire, gave it a warm welcome. Allison Rieck put her keen mind to it, with a dose of purging and strengthening medicine and some editorial vitamins.

As always, deep gratitude is due my husband, John Hoyte, and my family tribe for their love and support during times when I lost heart and needed reviving.

Notes

CHAPTER 2: THE FACES OF THE EARTH

[1]Willa Cather, *Death Comes for the Archbishop* (New York: Random House, 1990), 291.

CHAPTER 3: BEAUTY

[1]Annie Dillard, *The Living* (New York: Harper Perennial, 2013).

[2]Gerard Manley Hopkins, "Pied Beauty," *Poems and Prose of Gerard Manley Hopkins*, ed. W. H. Gardner (New York: J. M. Dent, 1979), 30.

[3]John Calvin, *Calvin's Commentaries*, trans. John King, vol. 8, *Psalms, Part I* (1847-1850), available online at www.sacred-texts.com/chr/calvin/cc08/index.htm.

[4]From "St. Romuald's Brief Rule," available online at www.camaldolese.com/information.html.

[5]Paul Mariani, in a personal conversation.

[6]Anonymous, *The Cloud of Unknowing* (Brewster, MA: Paraclete, 2009).

[7]John Calvin, quoted in *Calvin Today: Reformed Theology and the Future of the Church*, ed. Michael Welker, Ulrich Möller and Michael Weinrich (London: T&T Clark, 2011), 37.

CHAPTER 4: THE MARKINGS OF GRACE

[1]John Keats, "Ode on a Grecian Urn" (1819).

[2]C. S. Lewis, "The Day with a White Mark," *Poems* (London: Harcourt, 1994), 28.

[3]Quoted from a personal letter.

CHAPTER 5: DETERMINING IDENTITY

[1]David Grann, "The Mark of a Masterpiece," *New Yorker*, July 12, 2010, 51.

[2]Ibid.

[3]Ibid.

[4]From the poem "The Moths," in *New and Selected Poems* (Boston: Beacon Press, 1992), 132.

[5]See contemplativeoutreach.org.

[6]Frederick Buechner, *Wishful Thinking: A Theological ABC* (New York: Harper & Row, 1973).

CHAPTER 6: INDELIBLE IMPRESSIONS

[1]Flannery O'Connor, *Everything That Rises Must Converge* (New York: Farrar, Straus & Giroux, 1965).

CHAPTER 7: SEALS OF AUTHENTICITY

[1]*The Book of Common Prayer* (New York: Seabury Press, 1979), 623.

CHAPTER 8: REMARKING, REMAKING

[1]Gerard Manley Hopkins, "Pied Beauty," *The Major Poems*, ed. Walford Davies (London: Dent & Sons, 1979), 68.

[2]George Herbert, "The Elixir," *George Herbert and the Seventeenth-Century Religious Poets*, ed. Mario A. Di Cesare (New York: Norton, 1978), 65.

[3]Richard Rohr in a homily at The Glen Workshop, St. John's College, Santa Fe, New Mexico, August 2014.

CHAPTER 9: SCARS AND STAINS

[1]*The Book of Common Prayer* (New York: Seabury Press, 1979), 360.

CHAPTER 11: A SAD, SMEARED PRINT

[1]Collect, *The Book of Common Prayer* (New York: Oxford University Press, 1990), 360.

CHAPTER 12: GOD-PRINTED PEOPLE

[1]Poem first published in Luci Shaw, *Harvesting Fog* (Montrose, CO: Pinyon, 2010), 64.

List of Poems

"Paul's Thorn." In *The Englewood Review* 4, no. 4 (2014).

"Prism." In *Harvesting Fog*. Montrose, CO: Pinyon, 2010.

"Rising, the Underground Tree." In *Accompanied by Angels*. Grand Rapids: Eerdmans, 2006.

"Soft Rock." In *Scape*. Eugene, OR: Cascade, 2013.

"Suspended."

"Tenting, Burr Trail, Long Canyon, Escalante." In *What the Light Was Like*. Seattle: Wordfarm, 2006.

"To the Edge." In *Harvesting Fog*. Montrose, CO: Pinyon, 2010.

"Two Stanzas: The Eucharist." In *Polishing the Petoskey Stone*. Vancouver, BC: Regent College Publishing, 2003.

Also by Luci Shaw

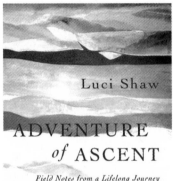

Adventure of Ascent
978-0-8308-4310-7